Female Parts

To Elizabeth and Audrey

Female Parts

The Art and Politics of Women Playwrights

Yvonne Hodkinson

BLACK
ROSE
BOOKS

Montréal/New York

BLACK ROSE BOOKS No. V168

Hardcover ISBN: 0-895431-07-7
Paperback ISBN: 0-895431-06-9

Canadian Cataloguing in Publication Data

Hodkinson, Yvonne, 1962
Female parts
ISBN 1-895431-07-7 (bound) – ISBN 1-895431-06-9 (pbk.)

   1. Canadian drama (English)—Women authors—History and criticism.
2. Canadian drama (English)—20th century—History and criticism.
I. Title.

PS8089.5.W6H63 1991   C812'.5408'09287   C91-090493-6
PR9188.H63 1991

Library of Congress No. 91-72977
Cover Design: Werner Arnold

Editorial Offices
BLACK ROSE BOOKS
3981 St-Laurent Blvd.
Suite 444
Montréal, Québec
H2W 1Y5 Canada

Mailing Address
BLACK ROSE BOOKS
P.O. Box 1258
Succ. Place du Parc
Montréal, Québec
H2W 2R3 Canada

BLACK ROSE BOOKS
340 Nagel Drive
Cheektowaga, New York
14225 USA

Contents

Introduction

With the burgeoning of the feminist movement in the past two decades, women playwrights in many countries have begun articulating a new voice in theatre. But in Canada, the pursuit of a female vision is unique in that it examines the notion of gender and female identity through the lens of cultural mythology. Although writers such as Margaret Atwood, Alice Munro and Margaret Laurence have probed the relationship between female and national identity in fiction, and have been the topic of research by critics like Marian Fowler and Coral Ann Howells, this study offers the first critical attempt to place women playwrights in a Canadian literary context in which "myths and legends of landscape"[1] symbolize self-discovery and the quest for an aesthetic as well as a socio-political feminized space.

This book explores the creative contribution to dramatic literature of Margaret Hollingsworth, Aviva Ravel, Antonine Maillet, Betty Jane Wylie and Cindy Cowan, focusing on six plays which dramatize Canadian cultural mythology from the standpoint of the female imagination: *Ever Loving* and *Islands* by Margaret Hollingsworth; *The Twisted Loaf* by Aviva Ravel; *La Sagouine* by Antonine Maillet; *A Place on Earth* by Betty Jane Wylie, and *A Woman From the Sea* by Cindy Cowan.

Although the work of many other playwrights, like Sharon Pollock, Beverley Simons, Elinore Siminovitch, Judith Thompson, and others, could have been included in this analysis, the scope of this study prevented me from including all of them. However, in the first chapter, "Restaging the Past," reference is made to the many women playwrights who developed a feminist awareness in Canadian theatre over the decades.

The six plays were selected because together they create a synthesized vision which reflects both a feminist aesthetic and a national consciousness. In their search for identity, these playwrights have transformed the literary myth of wilderness, the struggle for survival as immigrant, and the dominance of colonialism into a dramatic female mythology. By identifying 'wilderness' as the metaphorical female psyche, the 'immigrant' as a symbol of women's sense of marginality, and the 'colonial', 'imperial' mentality as suppression through patriarchal tradition, these playwrights add a new dimension to modern Canadian drama in the context of the search for national identity.

The plays, written in the 1970s and 1980s, represent the emergence of women playwrights on the Canadian dramatic scene at a period when the feminist movement was a potent influence on the awareness of women writers. The selected plays exemplify the creative consciousness of Canadian women playwrights and stress the need for a critical study that places their work in both a literary and feminist framework.

It will be demonstrated that although the exploration of regional characteristics has occurred frequently in Canadian drama, these five playwrights use regionalism to represent a female consciousness. Regional tendencies in Canadian drama have become symbolic representations of cultural myths, the "unchartered 'iconography of the imagination.'"[2] Thus, regionalism to these women playwrights is related to female identity, as the setting becomes a metaphor for the unexplored territory of the female imagination.

The discovery of the inner psyche is the focus, and the external setting becomes a backdrop for the internal landscape and the realization of a female sense of place. In addition, while these six plays are realistic on many levels, they also experiment with dramatic structure in their depiction of the fragmented, changing consciousness of many of their female protagonists. The characters in the plays express the psychological and emotional struggle of their search for self-identity through the use of monologue, flashbacks and the breakdown of time and space. Fragmented and experimental techniques are applied as a metaphor for the inner emotional and psychological state of flux.

Ever Loving and *Islands* explore the female inner self in connection with the inherited colonial tradition and the inherited patriarchal tradition. Women's sense of isolation and the need for self-recognition relate to both the national struggle for identity in the post-colonial age and the female struggle for identity in the traditions of patriarchy. These plays reveal how women playwrights explore the association of national identity and female identity on many levels. The portrayal of the immigrant is used to further emphasize the female sense of isolation and marginality. As foreigners, the female immigrants in *Ever Loving* are severed from their roots and must struggle in an unfamiliar setting. They are shown to be marginalized in two ways: as immigrants and as women.

In *Islands*, the protagonist withdraws to a secluded island in British Columbia. Escaping from social expectations, she isolates herself from human companionship and must battle alone with the incertitude of her existence as a woman and the uncertainties of the wilderness upon which she projects her process of self-discovery.

The immigrant concept is portrayed in *The Twisted Loaf* where an old Russian-Jewish woman, on the verge of death, reflects upon her life of struggle and self-sacrifice for her family in a new and foreign country. In solitude, the old woman achieves a meaningful connection with her past and a deeper understanding of her difficult responsibilities as a Russian-Jewish immigrant, wife and mother.

In *A Place on Earth*, the dramatic use of monologue is used to express the process of self-discovery, as an elderly rape victim strives for survival in an urban wilderness. The old woman's sense of exclusion and oppression is symbolized by her lonely rooming house and her only source of contact—a puppet she talks to. The struggle for autonomy is portrayed as her decision to press charges on her attacker, thus confronting her external environment.

In *La Sagouine,* a poor washerwoman becomes an expression of dignity and pride in the middle of hardship and oppression. Set in Acadia, the play adds a further dimension to women's quest for integration by incorporating language and religion into the experience of isolation and exclusion. As a French Canadian, the protagonist's struggle for meaning is magnified by her subservient position in a predominantly English society.

In *A Woman From the Sea,* mythology and ritual are used to connect the protagonist in the play with women's creative past, thus expressing the female playwright's search for her own dramatic roots. The ancient imagery of woman as a symbol of the life process is revealed, in conjunction with the dramatic use of fertility rituals, "the origins of drama,"[3] when women created dramatic rituals and played the part of the Mother Goddess.

Canadian women playwrights are in the process of "writing themselves into existence,"[4] a term used by Robert Wallace to describe the artistic consciousness of Canadian dramatists. When applied to women, this term has special significance, as women are only beginning to dramatize their personal visions in theatre. By writing themselves into existence, Canadian women playwrights are charting out new territory in the realm of drama and feminist thought. By creating this map, they are developing the "tools of analysis"[5] that will enable women to recognize a female consciousness from within an aesthetic and national framework.

NOTES

1. Howells, Coral Ann. *Private and Fictional Words: Canadian Women Novelists of the 1970s and 1980s,* London and New York: Methuen, 1987. p. 30.
2. Wagner, Anton. quoting James Reaney in "Introduction" to *Contemporary Canadian Theatre: New World Visions,* ed. Anton Wagner, Toronto: Simon and Pierre, 1985, p.16.
3. Malpede, Karen. ed. *Women in Theatre: Compassion and Hope,* New York: Drama Books Publishers, 1983, p.5.
4. Wallace, Robert. "Writing the Land Alive: The Playwrights' Vision in English Canada," *Contemporary Canadian Theatre,* Conolly, ed. p. 80.
5. Lushington, Kate. "Fear of Feminism," *Canadian Theatre Review,* 43, (Summer 1985) p. 10.

I

Restaging the Past

Ever since Confederation, Canada as a nation has been struggling with the question of identity. In parallel development, the 19th century quest for a national identity gave impetus to a new feminist consciousness. Concomitant with the national urge to find self-definition, and to be free from the yoke of British imperialism, a feminist awareness began to evolve which demanded recognition in a strongly paternalistic society. Women like Dr. Emily Howard Stowe, Emily Willoughby Cummings and Lady Ishbel Aberdeen, president of the National Council of Women of Canada, began to examine the dichotomy between woman's private sphere as homemaker, and the exclusively masculine control of the public world.

Although the early supporters of women's emancipation reflected all the optimism and hope of a new nation, and believed that women's contribution to social reform would secure a more just, united country, the greater part of Canadian society remained unaffected by the thrust of change and clung inexorably to the traditions of the past. The perception of influential men like the Reverend Robert Sedgwick epitomizes the fear of liberated women usurping "the place of man," a position she "was not designed to fill."[1]

The stubborn belief in the traditions of the past prevented change from occurring at a rapid pace. This was most evident in drama where plays depicting Canadian subjects were superseded by the more popular British plays. When it came to a Canadian perspective that was also feminist, playwrights were fighting against two powerful traditions. Nevertheless, women of the 19th century did manage to write plays expounding a feminist vision; one such woman was Eliza Lanesford Cushing (1794-1886). Although her play *The Fatal Ring* is set in France, it expresses the awareness of female oppression by patriarchal rule, represented in the play as the corruption of the French court and the king who ravishes and socially ruins the protagonist, Estelle. Through Estelle, Cushing creates the first tragic heroine found in Canadian women's plays and "the first tragic hero in English-Canadian drama."[2]

Although the playwright lacks the awareness of a national identity, her writing expresses the need to define a female consciousness. By making her character withdraw from society to a convent, her only refuge after her husband abandons her, the playwright explores the discovery of self, separate from social obligation and marriage. The recognition of Estelle's individuality and need for self-growth introduces the beginning of a feminist vision in Canadian drama.

Cushing's plays, called "poetic dramas," like the poetic dramas of the Romantic poets, were meant to be read. Because of this, Cushing was frequently able to publish her work in the prestigious *Literary Garland*, achieving wide critical acclaim by her contemporaries. The editor of the *Garland*, John Gibson, had this to say about Cushing: "The ease and fluency, as well as the unity of plot, and felicity with which this gifted authoress traces out the denouement of her tales, command the admiration and interest of every reader."

Another 19th century playwright who demonstrates a female awareness is Sarah Anne Curzon, (1833-1898) who, like Cushing, wrote poetic dramas depicting strong female heroines. Yet Curzon's heroines are less tragic and more independent than that of Cushing's. With her play, *Laura Secord, the Heroine of 1812*, Curzon becomes the first playwright to explore a clear definition of female identity in relation to a national consciousness. By portraying the historical figure of Laura Secord, who was instrumental in saving Upper Canada from an American invasion, Curzon spotlights the forgotten women of history who helped develop the nation. As a playwright she is also significant in that she is the first to question traditional gender roles. When Laura's husband is wounded on the battle field, she courageously marches off through the dark wilderness, in the middle of the approaching battle, to warn the Lieutenant of the planned American attack on Upper Canada, "a task at which a man might shrink."[3] By facing the unknown, the heroine attempts to assert herself in the world around her. In a metaphorical sense, by fighting her way through the dark forest, the heroine confronts the limitations of her environment. By giving Laura the conventional male attributes of courage and valour, and her husband James the traditional female position of dependency and helplessness, the playwright challenges notions of gender stereotyping.

In her *Preface* to the play, published in 1887, Curzon expresses the need to appreciate the great deeds of Canadian women. Through Laura Secord, Curzon creates a symbol of female autonomy and empowerment within a political and aesthetic framework. "To set her on such a pedestal of equality; to inspire other hearts with loyal bravery such as hers; to write her name on the roll of Canadian heroes, inspired the poem that bears her name."

As an active member of the Toronto Women's Literary Club and the President of the Women's Canadian Historical Society, Curzon was politically involved in the emancipation of Canadian women. Her play, *The Sweet Girl Graduate*, satirizes women's exclusion from universities. Again, the accepted roles of gender are confronted when the protagonist, Kate, obtains a Master of Arts degree and top honours in math, science and the classics, proving that "Canadian girls are equal in mental power with Canadian boys."

Working both actively and artistically to improve the position of women, Curzon's play, *The Sweet Girl Graduate*, along with her political speeches, contributed to a change in women's status. In 1884, two years after the play was published, women were admitted to University College for the first time. Also in that year, unmarried women who possessed property were given the right to vote in municipal elections in Toronto. Yet it was not until 1917, 19 years after Curzon's death, that women were granted the vote in the provincial elections of Ontario, followed by the vote in federal elections in 1920. Although it was not until 1940 that Quebec women were allowed to vote, finally enfranchising all Canadian women.

Another 19th century and early 20th century playwright who fostered the artistic and feminist development of Canada is Catherine Merritt, (1859-1926). In her work, Canada is seen as a land of hope and opportunity to the newly arrived Empire Loyalists from America. Her play, *When George the Third Was King,* based on the life of her great-great-grandfather, is an idealistic view of pioneer life in 18th century life. The main significance of the play is the heroine's coherent vision of national identity projected 100 years into the future. Her foresight represents the expansion of women's consciousness in conjunction with social progress. The utopian vision of the Canadian wilderness grips the female imagination as Merritt links human potential to the inexhaustible landscape.

The impulse toward new possibilities also inspired the rejection of old forms, for it was out of this new faith, mirrored in the surroundings, that Canada began to distance itself from Britain. But shaking off the Empire's influence proved to be a difficult task, one that Canadian's early women playwrights felt most of all. For these women wrote in a society that was patriarchal in its political and cultural structure. Like Britain, Canada's legal system excluded women from voting and from taking part in parliament and the court of law; all women's possessions, including property and her children, belonged to her husband by law. As a colony of Britain, Canada inherited these male-centred traditions, along with British cultural and literary models.

But ironically, being connected to Britain led to the challenging of patriarchy and the assertion of women's rights. For it was in Britain that the women's movement originated, giving Canadian women the inspiration to fight for equality. However, in the New World, the Canadian suffragette movement took a different form from its British counterpart. Propelled by the excitement of nationalism, women like Nellie McClung envisioned the positive social repercussions of women's emancipation. Through actively participating in society, women would help develop an independently strong Canada. McClung wrote in 1914:

> We would re-write our history. We would copy no other country. We would be ourselves, and proud of it. How we scorned the dull brown Primer from which we had learned Canadian history! Written as it was from the top down with no intimate glimpses of the people at all.[4]

It was this very quest for an original voice which generated the need for Canadian drama. Through the creation of hundreds of community and little theatres throughout the country, a Canadian identity began to emerge. Most of the Canadian plays at this time were part of the amateur theatre movement, whereas the professional theatres produced mainly British and American imports. As a result of the colonial age, people looked to Britain for cultural and dramatic standards. The idea of possessing an indigenous drama did not seem possible. In his 1928 article entitled "Nationalism and Drama," Merrill Denison writes, "Either it is colonial or American. In a discussion of the theatre, it does not seem to matter much which. In either case the possibilities of a native drama are nil."

In developing this indigenous drama, women took part as playwrights, actresses and directors within the many local communities and little theatres. One of these theatres was the Vancouver Little Theatre, which fostered the production of Canadian playwrights like Mary Reynolds in the 1920s, who later won the 1936 New Frontier playwrighting competition.

In the 1930s, women like Dora Smith Conover and Leonora McNeilly of the Canadian Women's Press Club, saw the importance of producing a national drama. Through the establishment of the Playwright's Studio Group in Toronto in 1932, these women forged an important stronghold

9

through which Canadian drama could flourish. The Studio Group also became a place for female playwrights to discover an aesthetic consciousness.

Elizabeth Haynes co-founded the Banff School of Fine Arts in 1933 and the Edmonton Little Theatre where playwrights like Gwen Pharis Ringwood and Elsie Park Gowan emerged. Haynes also helped to generate the community drama movement in Alberta, when there was no CBC in the Prairies, no little theatres and no university drama programmes. Another pioneer, Dora Mavor Moore, who founded the New Play Society in Toronto, did much to develop Canadian theatre by dedicating her career to training young actors, directors and playwrights.

Playwright Lois Reynolds Kerr, after winning a national drama competition for her labour drama, *Open Doors,* in 1930, became part of the Playwright's Studio Group. Her plays satirize the frivolous pursuits of the middle class at a time of national crisis during the Depression. Three of her plays, *Among Those Present, Nellie McNabb* and *Guest of Honour* are significant in that they reveal the stereotyped behaviour of women trapped in a limited society with no option other than to marry a man of status. Kerr's comic vision is the expression of the social milieu she observed as a society news journalist and her plays were directed at audiences seeking relief from the dreariness of the Depression. Critic John Holden believed people in the 1930s preferred to see light-hearted comedies rather than well-acted tragedies or "morbid" plays. "To bring the theatre back, you must give the people comedy."[5]

Perhaps the economic Depression which tempted people to evade social reflection also prevented women from questioning their position in Canadian society. The pursuit of national identity meant the defining and recognition of the harsh economic realities, just as the search for a female voice meant the painful acknowledgement of women's lack of power in society.

Canadian playwrights were writing plays that penetrated the social fabric of the Depression, but they were not well received by Canadian audiences. Workers' theatre groups sprung up all over the country, advocating political change for the working class, and at the same time experimented with theatrical conventions. One of the most famous was the Worker's Experimental Theatre in Toronto. In their attempt to fight for social justice, husband and wife founders Oscar and Toby Ryan also created plays which attacked British and American imperialism. Plays such as *Solidarity* and *Eight Men Speak* did much to establish an original Canadian theatre based on the every day lives of workers throughout the country. In this period of social change, however, it is surprising that no plays were written articulating the situation of women and the need for an assessment of their social status. Only the difficult conditions of the male workers became material for plays.

The female experience of the Depression was not explored until 1938 when Gwen Pharis Ringwood wrote *Still Stands the House,* followed by *Dark Harvest* in 1939. However, *Dark Harvest* had to wait until 1945 to be produced, as audiences in the Depression years were not ready to acknowledge the tragic truth it presented. Writing from a socialist awareness, Ringwood is the first Canadian playwright to portray the harsh realities of the prairies from a female point of view. In her plays the isolation and marginalized position of women is reflected in the prairie landscape. In *Dark Harvest,* wilderness is associated with the disintegration of the female character Hester, whose inner turmoil is magnified by the relentless blizzard of the prairie winter. Women's place in the prairie setting is linked to her situation in the patriarchal system: both are expressions of a man's world. *Still Stands the House* and *Dark Harvest* both depict women's lives on the Canadian prairie from an original perspective; one that honestly portrays their frustration and lack of control over their own lives. In a modern context, Ringwood's plays provide a foundation for feminist thought in Canadian drama, and suggest the need for a transformation of women's place in the patriarchal tradition.

In the 1940s and 50s, Elsie Park Gowan and Patricia Joudry found an outlet for their female consciousness in CBC radio drama. In Gowan's 1940

11

play, *The Hungry Spirit*, the heroine breaks from convention by refusing to marry in order to fulfill her life-time dream of becoming a scientist. Joudry's 1952 play, *Mother is Watching*, shows how two sisters uphold the debilitating social mores of the 1950s, while a third sister lives a life free from social expectations and stereotypes.

As the 20th century progressed and the recognition of Canadian culture developed, so too did women's position in society. The main concern of women in the 19th and early 20th century was to change the legal status of women. But once the vote for women was obtained in 1920, the women's movement seemed to lose impact. What needed to be changed were the social and psychological patterns which oppressed women, and it was not until the 1960s that women began confronting these issues on a wide scale. Ringwood's *Lament for Harmonica*, (1959) about the exploitation of an Indian woman, marks the approaching feminist vision which was to gain impetus throughout the 60s decade.

Books like *The Feminine Mystique* (1961) and *Sexual Politics* (1967) gave momentum to the latent women's movement throughout the world, and galvanized women into questioning a society that rendered them politically and socially powerless. Motivated by this new expression of feminism, women writers began to transfer notions of gender into their aesthetics. Canadian women playwrights emerged on the artistic scene in increasing numbers, integrating feminist sensibility with dramatic forms. Beverley Simons, Mary Mitchel and Aviva Ravel were three such playwrights who probed the female psyche in their work. In this revolutionary context, the 1960s produced an aesthetic awakening which made Canadian audiences more receptive to the omnipresent female vision. Beverley Simons' *Crabdance* (1969) burst on the scene with a controversial portrayal of an elderly woman. This play paved the way for more authentic depictions of women which included the negative feelings of anger, frustration and a yearning for change. Yet it was not until the 1970s that the female playwright's imagination came into fruition on a national scale. These playwrights brought to the stage an originative drama seeped in the cultural excitement and social change of the time.

As part of the nationalistic movement in Quebec, French women playwrights like Denise Boucher, author of *Les Fées Ont Soif*, presented a world in which women were stifled by domestic misery and endless child-bearing. What distinguishes French Canadian playwrights most from their Anglophone counterparts is their perception of patriarchy. To the Francophone playwright, patriarchy is the all powerful Catholic Church. The Anglophone playwright, Betty Lambert, growing up in the Catholic tradition, is one of the exceptions to that rule. *Jennie's Story* epitomizes the subjugation of women by the Catholic Church through the sexual abuse and sterilization of a 15 year old girl by the local priest. Based on a true story which occurred in the 1930s, the play embodies the religious control over women's bodies and the condemnation of female sexuality.

Many Anglophone playwrights like Lambert began their discovery by looking backwards. Diane Grant's *What Glorious Times They Had* (1974) recalls the feminist crusades of Nellie McClung; Carol Bolt's *Red Emma* (1974) brings the passionate 19th century American feminist, Emma Goldman, to the stage, and Wendy Lill's *Fighting Days* (1984) portrays the moral vision of the Manitoban suffragette, Francis Beynon. In *Blood Relations,* (1980) Sharon Pollock reinterprets the 19th century legend of Lizzie Borden, accused and later acquitted of murdering her father and step-mother. Ann Henry's *Lulu Street* (1972) attempts to understand female experience within the context of the 1919 Winnipeg General Strike. The play shows how although men were fighting the cause of the oppressed workers, they relied upon women's subservient roles in fulfilling their political goals. Mary Humphrey Baldridge's *The Photographic Moment* (1974) is a look back to the 1930s era when three sisters are forced into loveless marriages out of financial necessity and they struggle to keep their identity in a powerless situation. *Play Memory,* (1983) by Joanna M. Glass, describes how an abusive father in the Depression era controls the lives of his wife and daughter. Sharon Stearns, in *Sarah and Gabriel* (1979) explores

13

the quest for a meaningful past by interweaving the life of Gabriel, the wife of legendary womanizer, Luke Dawes, with the present life of Sarah, a contemporary film-maker. Sarah soon finds there is more legendary significance in the character of his wife Gabriel, thereby recognizing the excluded women in Canadian history and the need to define their position in the modern world.

Plays such as these express the historical entrapment of women in a male-oriented society, but do so in an attempt to comprehend female experience in a modern context. It is revealing that so many feminist plays deal with historical settings and figures. Most of the playwrights begin with unravelling women's past as a first step to understanding present day Canadian women. In order to achieve a feminist affirmation of self, what Gerda Lerner calls "autonomy," women must move out "of a world in which one is born to marginality, to a past without meaning, and a future determined by others—into a world in which one acts and chooses, aware of a meaningful past and free to shape one's future."[6]

When women playwrights create plays dealing with a modern Canadian context, many explore the alienation and exclusion of women trapped in suburban and urban wastelands. Plays like Elinore Siminovitch's *Tomorrow and Tomorrow,* (1972) Mary Humphrey Baldridge's *Bride of the Gorilla,* (1974) Judith Thompson's *The Crackwalker,* (1980) Sharon Pollock's *Doc* (1984) and Pamela Boyd's *Inside Out* (1985) are all examples of women's separation from mainstream society and their misery in the domestic home becomes a metaphor for female isolation. In the feminist playwright's vision, poverty, fear, old age, and stereotyped sex roles represent the many faces of oppression which have kept women from becoming active participants in society.

Out of this recognition of oppression comes the shift towards self-actualization and control over one's surroundings. Plays like *The Lodge* (1974) by Gwen Pharis Ringwood, *Rites of Passage* (1975) by Cam Hubert and *A Woman From the Sea* (1986) by Cindy Cowan reaffirm women's connection

14

with nature and re-establish the important bonds which lead to a deeper understanding of their own existence.

The five playwrights in this study represent a growing awareness of artistic identity grounded in a firm recognition of place. Their plays articulate the estrangement and disorientation experienced by women, but they also capture the impulse toward self-realization rooted in a feminized space. Contemporary women playwrights are involved in the difficult process of making sense out of centuries of role models which give a distorted picture of women's lives. In a metaphorical sense, feminist playwrights must rewrite their scripts by uncovering and interpreting the voices and experiences of women. Only then will Canadian theatre reflect the integral perception of its playwrights. Drama becomes a stimulating medium to carry out this endeavour, as it journeys from the personal realm to the public arena. In this public arena, women's presence must be recognized and consolidated. The stage, as a metaphor for the world, becomes the setting in which women project their vision, enabling women to move out of the silent margins into a vocal celebration of life.

NOTES

1. Cited in *The Proper Sphere: Woman's Place in Canadian Society,* Cook, Ramsay, and Wendy Mitchison, eds., Toronto: Oxford University Press, 1976. p. 9.
2. Wagner, Anton. *Canada's Lost Plays: Women Pioneers,* vol. 2, Toronto: Canadian Theatre Review Publications, 1979. p. 23.
3. Curzon, Sarah Anne. *Laura Secord, the Heroine of 1812,* Cited in *Women Pioneers,* p. 93.
4. McClung, Nellie. *The Stream Runs Fast,* 1945, reissued by Thomas Allen Ltd. 1965.
5. Holden, John. "Please, More Comedies," *Curtain Call,* 9, no.1, (October 1937) p. 4.
6. Lerner, Gerda. *The Female Experience,* Indianapolis: Bobbs-Merrill Co. Inc, 1977. p. xxxiv.

II

Ever Loving

Margaret Hollingsworth, through her exploration of the concepts of wilderness, the immigrant, and colonialism, delves into the complexities of Canadian female experience. Pivotal to her establishment as a key figure in Canadian drama is her scrutiny of cultural mythology in quest of a female aesthetic. Her plays articulate women's search for cultural, social and psychological identity in their struggle to achieve an external and internal sense of space.

Dislocation and the search for integration in Hollingsworth's plays are revealed through the metaphors of wilderness, in which the landscape symbolizes woman's individual incertitude, her isolation as immigrant in a foreign setting, and her low status in a male dominated society. Critics like Marian Fowler and Coral Ann Howells have discussed how Canadian women's fiction has transformed the myth of wilderness to represent a female consciousness.

The wilderness as the pathless image beyond the enclosure of civilized life was appropriated by women as the symbol of unmapped territory to be transformed through writing into female imaginative space.[1]

Margaret Hollingsworth explores in dramatic terms the relationship between the female imagination and the metaphorical images of wilderness. The heuristic effect of her perception of female isolation and displacement, and the search for individual locality is enhanced by Hollingsworth's own position as a playwright, a British immigrant, and as a woman.

> Home comes in again and again in my work. It's about relating to the place that you're in and finding a place for yourself in a foreign environment, which is what I'm doing. Feeling out of context, out of place, motivates me and informs my work.[2]

In *Ever Loving,* produced in 1980, Hollingsworth interweaves the complex issues of national identity, immigration, and female alienation, in relation to colonialism and the experience of the exile. Critics like John Moss use the term "colonial mentality"[3] to describe the dislocating effects experienced by the native-born Canadian. This results from "being born in exile, of accepting foreign experience as more valid, more relevant, than one's own."[4] The physical displacement of "immigrant exile,"[5] on the other hand, intensifies the feeling of being an outsider, of being subject to "conflicting orders, of alien conditions, of established chaos."[6]

Hollingsworth gives the colonial mentality and the immigrant exile concepts further significance by relating them to gender. The three men in *Ever Loving,* as native-born Canadians, are prey to feelings of inadequacy and dislocation in the face of British control and European influence. The women's sense of alienation, however, stems from their situation as immigrants which is further amplified by their marginal position in the structure of patriarchy.

Their overwhelming sense of being exiled from their familiar European setting is emphasized by the vastness of the landscape. The wilderness, the unchartered territory, is used by Hollingsworth as a backdrop against which feelings of apprehension and estrangement are played out in different ways. The impenetrable wilderness initially encroaches upon the individuality, the psychic sense of place, of all three women. Circumscribed by primeval nature, limited by colonial and patriarchal expectations, they must learn to cope with profound loss of self-esteem. Severed from their roots, they experience fragmented states of consciousness as they attempt to adapt to what they perceive as ostracism and banishment. Coral Ann Howells offers a succinct explanation of the female experience in patriarchy in relation to the imperial control of Canada.

> There are close parallels between the historical situation of women and of Canada as a nation, for women's experience of the power politics of gender and their problematic relation to patriarchal traditions of authority have affinities with Canada's attitude to the cultural imperialism of the United States as well as its ambivalence towards its European inheritance.[7]

As colonialism is an inherited tradition, and shown to be inadequate in defining the Canadian experience, so too can patriarchy be perceived as an inadequate and foreign tradition in defining the female experience. Thus the sense of effacement and dependency of the three women is increased by their immigrant status, and by their position dictated by "sexual politics." For, as Kate Millett observes, "status, temperament, and role are all value systems with endless psychological ramifications"[8] within the traditions of patriarchy.

Playwrights like Gwen Pharis Ringwood articulate the link between colonial domination and male control over women. *Lament for Harmonica*, (1959) by portraying the exploitation of a native woman by a white man, is the first play to associate imperial rule in Canada with patriarchal authority over women. Margaret Hollingsworth's play *Ever Loving* expands this vision of imperial male domination to represent the

multi-faceted psychological and social ramifications of female dislocation as experienced by three immigrant women in Canadian post-war
society. Three war brides, Luce, Ruth and Diana arrive in Canada after
the second world war to join their Canadian husbands. Although Luce
comes from Italy, Ruth from Scotland, and Diana from England, they
are excluded from the imperial power structures because they are
women. The husbands in the play, although they are shown to be victims of the colonial mentality as native Canadians, are able to identify
with the male hierarchy because of their superior position as men.

Hollingsworth's portrayal of the socio-political structures of patriarchy encompasses the essence of the 1970's feminist movement in which
female oppression and male dominance are perceived as the products of
mass "socialization."[9] Feminists like Kate Millett, Adrienne Rich and
Elizabeth Janeway claim that social conditioning has led to an ideology of
gender, a "social mythology" in which a set of beliefs dictate male and
female experience based on biology, guaranteeing "superior status in the
male, inferior in the female."[10]

In *Ever Loving*, Hollingsworth incorporates the feminist search for
definition with the Canadian literary search for identity. The archetype of
the 'immigrant as exile', so prevalent in Canadian literature with writers
like Brian Moore and Henry Kreisel, has come to express a national sense
of alienation, for there is a sense that, as Atwood claims, "we are all
immigrants to this place even if we were born here..."[11] In *Ever Loving*,
Hollingsworth affiliates the displacement of the immigrant in a foreign
country with the denial of female authenticity in a male dominated environment, thereby infusing sexual politics into the depiction of
"national exile."[12]

The play has often been compared with John Murrell's *Waiting for the
Parade*, but where Murrell's play is about the isolation of women left at
home when their husbands go off to war, Hollingsworth's play deals with
the complexities of trying to feel at home in an alien land, and more
significantly, with the socio-political fabric of patriarchy.

The structure of the play develops in an unchronological fashion. The breakdown of time and space and the shift from one woman's experience to another, create a fragmented perception of the three women's development in Canadian society. The play begins in 1970 with the established lives of Ruth, Diana and Luce as they are gathered together in a restaurant in Niagara Falls for the first time since their arrival in 1945. On the surface, the three women have achieved very different identities in Canadian society. Diana appears to have been assimilated into Canadian life, and talks of soon retiring to the West Coast with her husband, Paul, because the milder temperature is better for his "old war wound." (35) Ruth lives with Dave in Hamilton where he is a security officer. Nothing is revealed of Luce at this stage. She is shown sitting at a table alone while her former husband, Chuck, sings. Through the dinner conversation of the two couples, the external reality begins to fade as the memories of the past visualize into being.

DIANA: Well…it's been a long time eh? A heck of a time. Too long of course…Yes…well, nothing comes easily does it? I can't say I'd've changed anything though—looking back. It's extraordinary really. I don't know where the years've gone. (37)

Through Diana's consciousness, the play shifts back to 1945. Luce, Diana and Ruth have just arrived in Canada. Luce sits at the train station in Halifax alone and waiting, and Ruth and Diana take the train to meet their husbands. The journey through the wilderness gives the women their first impression of Canada and leads them to reflect upon the future of their own lives in an unfamiliar setting.

DIANA: Fir trees.
RUTH: Aye. And do you know they're full of bears. Dave told me. I wonder what the cows eat? It's all trees.

21

DIANA: Lovely colours. They must be maples…See…those red ones.
           That's their national tree.
RUTH: National tree? [Thinks.] We've got the thistle.
DIANA: They call autumn fall.
RUTH: It feels…different. Creepy. Foreign. [Pauses, has no word to
           express her feelings.] Big.
DIANA: Don't look at it.
RUTH: I can't help it.
DIANA: [Irritated.] Well don't.
RUTH: Don't shout at me. [Pause. RUTH is near to tears.]
DIANA: [Sighs.] It's going to take time isn't it? Getting the hang
           of…[Makes an expansive gesture.] (39)

The wilderness becomes the first image in the female characters' im-
aginations, personifying their state of inner disarray, expressing their uncertainty in a foreign and male-oriented country. The image of wilderness
in the play takes on a double meaning. On an internal level, wilderness
personifies the disordered, unformed female self; one that is a reflection of
the women's inner emotional world. On an external level, wilderness is a
metaphor for the social world of male experience; one the women feel
overwhelmed by. As a backdrop for the women's inner world, the wilderness brings to the surface Ruth and Diana's subconscious feelings of anxiety
and fear, an experience Kreisel calls "the impact of the landscape on the
mind."[13] The boundless forest also seems to trigger the undiscovered elements of their own beings, and appears to illuminate a dark and mysterious
terrain within. Diana reveals how everything seems so "untouched." The
untamed nature surrounding them appears to offer limitless possibilities.
"Space. That's what Paul said. A blank page just waiting for us to write on.
[Shakes her head.] I thought I understood him." (41) Diana has an ambivalent perception of herself in her new environment: the forest is both
frightening and inspiring. It is all so rejuvenating after the horrors of war,
but it is also terrifying in its wildness and unfamiliarity.

It's all...untouched. London's horrible now...ugly. Here everything's so splendidly...untouched. No bombing... nothing destroyed...mile upon mile...well, there's nothing to bomb is there? There's no one to kill. (41)

Like the landscape, Diana's untapped inner resources remain untouched. In metaphorical terms, wilderness in the play expresses the undiscovered potential of female consciousness, one that is both terrifying and exciting. Diana finds nothing that is conformable; even the familiarity of war is not to be found here, for, ironically, there is nothing to destroy.

The immeasurable forest also fills Diana with doubt, as it also implies disorder and chaos. Northrop Frye writes about the "tone of deep terror in regard to nature,"[14] and how it affects the imagination.

The human mind has nothing but human and moral values to cling to if it is to preserve its integrity or even its sanity, yet the vast unconsciousness of nature in front of it seems an unanswerable denial of those values.[15]

Hollingsworth's depiction of the impact of wilderness on the human consciousness redefines Frye's analysis by combining the notion of gender. The threat of the wilderness accentuates the protagonists' feelings of vulnerability and dependency as women. They suddenly realize that they have little control over the development of their future lives placed in the hands of men they hardly know. The women are unable to articulate a sense of identity in their new environment, as Diana reveals. "It's going to take time isn't it? Getting the hang of...[Makes an expansive gesture.]" (39) To Ruth and Diana, the wilderness becomes a reflection of the male social environment in which they are without place and which they cannot fully comprehend. For just as they have no access to the trackless wilderness, they are powerless within the confines of their husbands' social environment.

Hollingsworth uses the fragmentation of language to emphasize the women's psychological displacement and lack of control. The landscape evokes feelings within the women which seem to surface for the first time; feelings that are so unfamiliar they cannot fully communicate them. Both Ruth and Diana try to convey their sense of disorientation through inarticulate images which reveal the lack of coherence of their inner worlds in relation to the outside world. Ruth tries to express her own perception but her thoughts, too, disintegrate into incoherent utterances. "...It's all so...so..." (42)

To escape from the feeling of helplessness evoked by the forest, Ruth and Diana cling to the security of domestic life. Ruth perceives the retreat into the domestic realm as a refuge. "Oh, it'll be all right—as soon as I see Dave—as soon as I see my house. He's going to love Rita." (39-40) Diana also escapes into the sanctuary she imagines marriage will be. "They'll be waiting for us—as long as we love them nothing else matters." (42)

The reliance on romantic love and the refuge of domesticity is a reiteration of the feminist claim that women, by internalizing male propaganda, have helped to maintain their exclusion from public society. In so doing, Janeway observes, women have "bought in" to the social mythology whereby they trade "private power in return for public submission."[16] This, she explains, is the "orthodox bargain" men make with women to ensure the continuation of male rule. The home in the patriarchal tradition becomes a woman's only source of power. For Ruth and Diana, this belief in the comfort and security of domesticity is a refuge from the outside world in which they have no place. However, all three women find their husbands do not offer protection and security, but isolation and domestic oppression. Ruth has come to Canada with the intention of assimilating into Dave's world. She finds, however, that Dave is without a job and they are forced to live in his mother's house. Dave is uncomfortable around the new baby and sees her as Ruth's responsibility. When Ruth tells him about her three A.M. feedings, he replies, "Well, just as long as you do it quietly." (75)

The play shifts back in time from the train ride in 1945 to the three women's lives in Europe prior to, and during the war. The year is 1938, and Ruth, Diana and Luce reflect upon the future of their lives. The shared consciousness of the three women is explored as the structure of the play dissolves into inner reflections through overlapping dialogue. Ruth reveals her secret desires for romantic love. "When I get married, I'll have a bedroom with a dressing table with three mirrors…" (47) The use of inner monologue and stream of consciousness expresses the private, emotional level of female experience, adding a dimension of fantasy to the realism of the play. By revealing her inner world, Diana shows that her daydreams are without focus. On one level, she dreams about the excitement of being a pilot, like her brother. "Now Hugh's been called up…I wouldn't mind being a pilot, if he can do it why can't I?" (46) She then slips into dreaming about foreign men, and the excitement they offer, like the men she met in Heidelberg. "…frightfully…masculine…in that sort of…German way." (47) Both Ruth and Diana's retreat into romantic love exemplifies the feminist notion that romantic love, as "the pivot of women's oppression,"[17] prevents women from achieving a state of autonomy. Luce, on the other hand, believes in her own destiny, and states, "I want to go to America!" (47) where she believes she can become a singing star.

The three women express different levels of female experience: Ruth exemplifies female identity waiting to be shaped by male experience, as she associates inner fulfillment with obtaining a husband. Luce represents the potential for female autonomy and the belief in individuality outside the boundaries of social expectations. Diana displays characteristics of both women. She possesses the desire to develop her potential, but she retreats into dreaming about exotic men as a way of achieving her identity. Ruth and Diana's inability to construct an reality outside romance expresses Shulamith Firestone's depiction of "inauthentic"[18] female experience, distorted by patriarchal conditioning.

When Diana meets Paul in England in 1941, she is intrigued by the fact that he is a communist and wants to end "bourgeois tyranny." (51) Paul personifies the excitement of the exotic and foreign which Diana longs for, expressing Canadian nationalist sentiment and the rebellion against colonial domination. "When this war's over there's a few things gonna change...it's the end of imperialism, all that stuff's dead. Canadians aren't licking any more boots..." (52) Although Paul envisions an end to tyranny, he does not include the power structures of patriarchy as part of imperialism. Nor does he question the limitations of patriarchy in his search for Canadian freedom from imperialism.

Hollingsworth echoes the insight of Susan Mann Trofimenkoff who claims that because nationalism is "a political idea,"[19] within the patriarchal framework, it has historically excluded women. Trofimenkoff shows how historians like Carl Berger focus on Canadian nationalism within a pastoral and patriarchal context.

> These men saw wheat and soldiers springing full grown out of the Canadian prairies. It did not occur to them that the evolution of liberty and self-government, so much admired, might entail women. Nor did they spot any women among the factories and the slums of the industrial order they so much despised.[20]

As Canadians fighting the war, Chuck, Dave and Paul see their country as the land of opportunity within the pastoral dream, a recurring theme in the Canadian imagination, what Frye perceives as "the nostalgia for a world of peace and protection, with a spontaneous response to the nature around it."[21] Paul's enthusiasm sparks Diana's imagination as she herself is searching for excitement. But as she lacks self-awareness and has no authentic goals of her own, this leads her to live vicariously through men like Paul. Diana tells Paul that she wanted to be a pilot in the WAF, so she could explore the Amazon, but her mother convinced her to join the police force as it was "safer." Diana had been enrolled in a secretarial college hoping to become a foreign secretary, but the school closed down during the war. She is desperate to get away from England and find something meaningful in her life. "I mean who wants to stick around here all their life?" (50)

When Diana meets Paul three years later, in 1944, he proposes marriage to her. She realizes that marrying Paul and going to Canada would mean breaking ties with her family and eradicating her past. "I can't. You don't understand. They'd never forgive me. My parents...I could never come back here." (72) But Diana does marry Paul, thereby giving up her past identity. Although Diana is afraid of severing the ties with her family, she also sees marriage to Paul and emigration to Canada as a means of escaping the limitations of her social milieu.

To all three women Canada represents the chance to start a new life. But Canada, with its colonial connection to Britain, is equally dominated by patriarchal tradition. For the women characters, Canada becomes the inversion of the pastoral myth. Contrary to the male immigrant's quest for prosperity through conquering the land, what Frye refers to as "the vision of a social ideal,"[22] Ruth and Diana are drawn to Canada by their belief in the myth of eternal marital happiness; hence the title "Ever Loving." Both Ruth and Diana's pastoral image of Canada embraces the myth of romantic love. The women come to Canada hoping they have found "prince charming" and will live "happily ever after" in a land of peace and protection. So for Ruth and Diana, the vast unspoilt Canadian environment exudes opportunity and escape from constraint. However, the desire for escape ends in further confinement, because the pastoral myth and the quest for "opportunity" sought in the New World is designated for men. Thus all three women in Canada find themselves assuming their husbands' identities and their social status.

Like Diana, Ruth also meets her future husband, Dave, in 1941. Ruth is in England pruning bushes as part of the war effort, when she meets Dave who paints an idyllic portrait of life in the Canadian wilderness. Ruth's imagination is fired by his description of endless summers at the cottage by a lake, and she starts to fantasize about Canada as the pastoral dream. She imagines an abundance of roses growing around their cottage door, and roasting a moose Dave trapped. Her pastoral dream is connected to romantic love, envisioning Dave as an adoring husband. "I can't take my hands off you. You're the best wife a man could have." (58)

Before they emigrate, Canada is a symbol of potentiality and opportunity. Luce, an upper-class young woman, dreams of going to America to become a singing star. To marry an American seems a way out of Luce's Italian sexist society where she has no sense of place. It is through Chuck, a Canadian of Italian descent, that Luce has the chance to discard her old identity and pursue her dream of becoming a singing star in New York. However, she is unaware that Canada is not part of the United States and that Halifax is a far cry from New York City. Luce is seduced by Chuck's description of Canada which incorporates the American dream of success with the myth of romantic love. "Canada's where it's happening. You better believe it. I'll show it to you, listen, I'll go and see your papa. Listen—you're gonna sing. You better do it over there." (65) Chuck then romantically puts his arm around Luce. "You're a nice quiet Italian girl, with a sense of humour. You're a beautiful girl, you know that?" (66) Luce falls for Chuck's glamorous depiction of Canada, igniting her desire to escape from the restrictive position of women in Italian society.

LUCE: Here women is making only bambini, more bambini! Is nothing other to make. In America...[Dreams herself into   perfect English.] For Christ's sake tell those people to stop following me...and there is no one can tell me I can't smoke. It is my voice. Mine. My apartment. My manager. I'm just too busy. And I don't give autographs! (47)

But what she does not realize is that Chuck also has a stereotyped view of women. Although he jokes about his father's advice: "You marry nice Italian girl, Carlo, you never have to clean your own shoes again," (65)

Chuck is shown to possess the same perception of wifely duties. Luce, instead of attaining the American dream of stardom, ends up in an Italian ghetto in Halifax living on top of her father-in-law's pizza business, confined to a one-room apartment where she is expected to be a traditional Italian wife.

Luce differs from the two other women immigrants in her belief that, through the American dream, she can achieve success as a singer. But as her perception of the American dream is intertwined with the myth of romantic love, she believes that she can attain her success by marrying an American. "I marry with American man. You come to bed, Yank?" (47) However, Luce's fantasy is short-lived, as she finds that marriage with Chuck entails submission to the conventional duties expected of a wife. She realizes she must reject both her patriarchal marriage and motherhood in order to become a success.

All three women find frustration and insecurity in their marriages, and are unable to adapt to their husbands' social setting. As in Mary Humphrey Baldridge's *Photographic Moment*, the unhappy marriages of the three women accentuate their loss of place. A manifestation of the 'immigrant exile' motif in Canadian literature, the female characters struggle against an environment that produces disappointment and failure. Atwood makes reference to the "swelling ranks of Canadian victims"[23] found in works like Adele Wiseman's *The Sacrifice*, John Marlyn's *Under the Ribs of Death*, and Brian Moore's *The Luck of Ginger Coffey*. As part of the immigrant's sense of alienation and exile, "Canada stands always ready not only to manufacture and export failure but to attract it and provide for it an appropriate setting."[24] What makes Margaret Hollingsworth's interpretation of the victimized immigrant is unique in that it is clearly linked to gender. For Ruth, Diana and Luce, failure is shown to be induced by their inferior positions as women, dominated by unambitious and parochial men. Paul sees Diana as the traditional farmer's 'help-mate', imagining her in his grandmother's apron baking her recipes for bread. Paul's pastoral utopia includes the identification with patriarchal power: the divine wisdom of the fathers.

Us and the land. I'm talking about the land. My father knew
that all the time—I wouldn't listen. Well, I'm listening now.
[Pause.] When you've been here a bit longer you'll see. It's
the key to Canada. This is peace... (77)

Like all three men in the play, Paul takes for granted that Diana will
accept his choices as her own. Just as he must conquer and mold the land,
so he assumes that he can shape Diana's identity. Illustrating the "Nature-
as-Woman"[25] metaphor in the Canadian literary imagination, Paul perceives the land as a "patient lover," (77) waiting to be shaped by male
experience. Henry Kreisel sees the exploitation and conquest of the land as
an expression of individual identity.

To conquer a piece of the continent, to put one's imprint
upon virgin land, to say, "Here I am, for that I came," is as
much a way of defining oneself, of proving one's existence,
as is Descartes' cogito, ergo sum.[26]

In a further analysis, Kreisel makes the analogy of conquering nature as an
act of rape:

The breaking of the land becomes a kind of rape, a passionate seduction. The earth is at once a willing and unwilling mistress, accepting and rejecting her seducer, the cause
of his frustration and fulfilment, and either way the shaper
and controller of his mind, exacting servitude.[27]

The breaking of the land, as a form of male dominance, is a way of
asserting the ego. Nature as woman exists to fulfill and replenish male
desire, and both nature and woman accept and reject their conqueror as
a "willing and unwilling mistress." It is only when 'Nature-Woman'
resists male power that she becomes unnatural, with "a sterile vir-

ginity "[28] associated with frigidity and death, like Hester in Ringwood's *Still Stands the House*, and Greta in Sheila Watson's *The Double Hook*.

To Diana, the male desire to dominate the land and produce fertile ground is a foreign idea, for all she sees is "Dead grass."(76) Forced to be part of the reality Paul has chosen, Diana sees the wilderness as a symbol of her dislocation and isolation. Cut off from her past, she is unable to find a sense of definition in a lifestyle not of her own choosing. "Anything else but not this—it's just wilderness." (77) Realizing that Paul is in a position of power over her, she becomes disturbingly aware of her own helplessness and entrapment. "I don't know what I'm going to do...please... please...I can't go back Paul. I'd never be able to hold my head up." (78) Hollingsworth's depiction of women's oppression in the prairie pastoral dream is an original restatement of Adrienne Rich's analysis of patriarchy as the "power of the fathers,"[29] whereby men determine women's fate in a socio-political, ideological and familial setting.

Paul, however, by his lack of success as a farmer, fails to live up to the traditions of the father he worships. Although Diana is without economic power, she is the one who has the ambition to make the farm a success, and it is she who does the manual labour on the farm when Paul would rather go bowling.

DIANA: I wanted to clean the truck tonight. I haven't had time to—we can't all sit around dreaming of the perfect farm. Somebody has to do the work! (82)

Diana longs to have a child, believing motherhood will give her the definition her life lacks. "If we don't then I... [Pause.] I don't see much point in slaving like this." (85) Unlike Luce whose rejection of motherhood increases her autonomy, Diana, stifled by her unfulfilled marriage, finds her childless position only increases her insularity.

Like Diana, Ruth comes to Canada hoping to find identity in the security of a happy domestic life. And similar to Diana, she finds that she

31

must adapt her husband's social milieu. But unlike Diana, Ruth passively accepts Dave's choices as her own without confrontation. She tries to make the best of life, but it is in moments of solitude that Ruth expresses her sense of exclusion and feelings of frustration.

> [Sits for a moment, looking after him.] Lose weight? You try losing weight when you're always pregnant. [To the door through which he left.] You don't have a girlfriend, do you Dave? Dave? (82)

By refusing to take Ruth out under the guise that she is too fat, Dave isolates her from the public realm and keeps her confined to the domestic world because she does not represent his idea of female beauty. By separating Ruth from external reality, Dave is guilty of fostering what Kathleen Storrie calls "social and psychological segregation."[30] Another form of Ruth's entrapment comes from Dave's stereotyped image of women, another "ancient instrument of containment,"[31] which keeps Ruth further cloistered in his limited perception of her. It is only when she is alone that Ruth asserts herself, expressing her helpless position in the home and her disbarment from the social realm of power to which Dave has free access.

Ruth's experience of motherhood as a form of oppression expounds the feminist notion that under patriarchy "motherhood as institution"[32] has undermined the possibility for female development. Through "the continuation of the species and the care of the home,"[33] women like Ruth are doomed to "immanence" and subject to male volition.

As in the Old World they left behind, the three protagonists find it is difficult to shake off the inherited traditions of patriarchy, discovering that they are sundered from the public realm and the power it bestows. Through their insularity, the women are united by a shared inner world where their verbal imagery becomes an expression of their private selves, separate from the outside worlds of their husbands.

DIANA: Don't go bowling tonight. [PAUL leaves.] You do still love
           me, Paul? Paul?
RUTH: You're not going out with someone else are you, Dave?
DIANA: The edge of the world. The edge... [Buries her face in her
           hands.]
RUTH: Don't leave me on my own.
LUCE: Why must I always be waiting? That is not why I came here.
           To wait. (83)

The partition of male/female experience in the play is related to the separation of "social landscape"[34] by what Kathleen Storrie terms "the ecology of gender."[35] The specific spacing of men and women has created what feminists like Kate Millett see as "two cultures,"[36] male and female, both inhabiting different psychological and social spheres.

As in her plays, *The Apple in the Eye* and *War Babies*, Hollingsworth explores the dichotomy of male/female realities—the external, unemotional world of the women's husbands, and the inner, private world the women escape to. The social landscape of Diana, Ruth and Luce is similar in that they are relegated to a powerless position separate from the external realm of male experience.

It is only Luce who is able to reject the conventions of patriarchy and begin to forge her own definition of selfhood in the New World. Only by breaking free from the isolation Chuck has placed her in does Luce begin to become part of Canadian society. By going to Toronto and becoming a media figure Luce succeeds in expanding the public/private boundaries, the "cultural dichotomy"[37] of male/female experience. Because Luce is not hindered by the myth of romantic love the way Ruth and Diana are, she identifies with her individual self, and not with the imposed perceptions of what she should be. But Luce's first seven years in Halifax were spent living a life determined by her husband, Chuck. She dreams of achieving her own independent status, meanwhile feeling trapped in a life over which she has no control. Luce had left Italy to escape from the patriarchal conception of women only to find herself stifled by the same definition. "I cannot to go back to Italy—there also they keep me in chains. I cannot to leave." (88)

The notion of race and class in relation to gender offers a further dimension to the three women's experiences in Canada. Ruth is from a working-class background and is shown to be more overwhelmed by her husband's power than is Diana or Luce. As a working-class woman, Ruth has less opportunity to acheive success in the outside world. Diana's upper-class background gives her the confidence to question her husband's authority, but not enough to repudiate his power. However, both Ruth and Diana are depreciated, although to different degrees, by their husbands' chauvinistic attitudes and the male power they take for granted.

Like Diana, Luce's upper-class background also leads her to question her husband's world, but it is her belief in herself as a singer that allows her to defy social expectations. Luce also feels there is "no culture" in her husband's parochial social milieu. But Luce articulates a deeper understanding concerning the limitations of her husband.

She touches on the notion that Chuck himself is shackled by the traditions of patriarchy and is unable to perceive Luce other than subject to himself.

LUCE: Many things I did not know how to say Chuck. No…was
not language. Not English, not Italian…how to make
you understand…How to make you hear when you do
not know how to listen. [Pause.] Not listen to words
but…[Reaches down inside herself, then gives up,
shrugs.] (92-93)

Luce also associates Chuck's inability to understand with the limiting of experience produced by colonialism, "the whole what you are is… Canadian."

The fact that Luce does not speak English well intensifies her sense of exclusion. She is also ostracized as an upper-class woman living amongst working-class Italians. Because Luce resists integration with her social setting, she is seen as an outsider and called a "fascist" by the Italian peasant immigrants.

Ruth and Diana, on the other hand, are in the privileged position of being linked to British influence, but because they are constrained by their patriarchal marriages, gender becomes their greatest barrier to integration into society. Although Luce is limited by nationality because she is not British, she is not impeded by notions of gender. As she is unfettered by society's definition of female experience, this allows her, unlike Ruth and Diana, to leave her stultified existence and search for success in Toronto. However, because Luce is not British, she must struggle for access into English Canadian society, and begins in the marginal position as a broadcaster on an Italian radio station.

John Moss writes about the "Anglophone exile"[38] as experiencing a distinct sense of dislocation different from other European immigrants:

> Their Canadian adaptation tends to appear as barbarous distortion, parody, ignorance, or contempt. His exile is further aggravated by the apparent indifference of the resident populace to the degeneration of values and desecration of ideals, as he sees them.[39]

The play augments this theory by revealing how the women's perception of Canadian society is influenced by gender. The women's apparent disdain for Canada stems from the frustration generated by their subordinate station as women bound to their husbands' low-ranking social positions. Both Luce and Diana's upper-class background makes them view Canadians as uncultivated and devoid of values. Luce has only contempt for Chuck and his native town of Halifax. "Is not even possible to drink wine in a restaurant, is possible smoke opium, but is not possible drink wine—is hypocrite town—no culture." (92) Diana finds Lethbridge without sophistication and the community without the will to develop. "If only somebody had a sense of humour! They're not even interested in local politics, in getting anything done. They seem to expect to suffer." (84) Ruth, on the other hand, does not criticize Canada's lack of culture or values, but, rather, scorns the unfriendliness and lack of joy she encounters. Her idea of happiness is tied to her warm memories of Scotland, as she finds Canadians, like Dave and the community of Hamilton, are without gaiety.

RUTH: We haven't been out in six months.
DAVE: Whose fault is that? Look at you—you should make friends.
RUTH: Who with? I can't even have people in…
              She…
DAVE: Ssssssh.
RUTH: Well, in Scotland you can just go and knock on anyone's door
              and they'll go down to the pub with you. You won't
              even dance now…In Scotland they're kicking up their
              heels 'til they're eighty. No one here even picks up a
              couple of spoons and clacks them. Where are your
              songs? (95)

As native-born Canadians, Chuck and Paul interpret their wives' criticisms of Canada as European superiority, perceiving the European foreigner as the prototypal "agent of imperial consciousness."[40] Chuck is threatened by Luce's disapproval of Canadian society: "You think you corner the market in sensibility because you're some high class dago bitch? Mussolini was an Italian." (93)

In her quest for self-realization, Luce finds inspiration through the affinity with successful actresses like Lotte Lenya and Marlene Dietrich. Chuck can only see these German actresses as a "bunch of spies," (88) saying that "Krauts aren't women." (88) He voices the inability to conceive a female definition of reality, an assumption that is clouded by a "male bias"[41] in the spectrum of patriarchy. Luce confronts this preconceived notion, "No...they are women. They are success." (88) Chuck discloses his antagonism towards Luce's pursuit of individuality by tearing up the pictures of the women she venerates. For what they represent most for Luce is an existence outside the domestic abode, separate from Chuck. This female parity signals the belief in a "female reality,"[42] as an alternative to the gender divided culture that has left women with a tenuous self-awareness, and envisions an end to female alienation through the alliance of women's universal recognition of a meaningful past.

Although careers as movie stars and singers can be considered stereotypical forms of success for women, the very act of achieving public recognition outside marriage and family disengages women, like Luce, from their conventional role.

Similar to Luce, Diana is propelled by the desire to succeed. She has great plans to go into fish farming and "change the economy of the region." (90) But Paul is made to feel inadequate by her inspirited self-motivation. He himself is unambitious and afraid to take risks and has cancelled their fish farming project without consulting Diana. Because Diana is without economic power, she is prevented from continuing the project alone.

As a way of evading his cowardice, Paul turns his attention towards the English flower seeds Diana has had imported from Britain, relating them to Diana's intrusion into the male domain of his prairie farm.

PAUL: Where did you get these?

DIANA: My mother sent them. I was planning to make a real English
           garden.

PAUL: You're not supposed to import seeds, you know that?

DIANA: Just a few flowers.

PAUL: It's the law. It's the law of this country...

DIANA: Since when were you such a great upholder of the law? (90)

On another level, the British seeds symbolize colonial interference, exposing Paul's own sense of insecurity as part of the colonial mentality,
whereby the individual feels alienated by "the force of an external
presence."[43] From Diana's perspective, by growing an English garden she
attempts to reshape the prairie wilderness to her own design. By cancelling
the fish farm and opposing her plans for a garden, Paul denies Diana any
form of power over the prairie farm. On the subject of women's public
power, Stacey and Price observe:

> Increased autonomy for women threatens men not only by
> the increased competition from women seeking to enter the
> public domain, but also by a decline in the support and ser-
> vices that they expect as individuals from women in their
> families.[44]

Diana affiliates her need to create a sense of place with the reclamation
of her British past. Thus the archetype of the British exile is given a further
dimension: As well as being a symbol of colonial domination to Paul, she
represents the threat of female intervention in the male world.

By creating her English country garden, Diana attempts to gain
control over what she perceives as the unnurtured Canadian wilderness.
By molding the landscape into the order of a country garden, Diana is at
the same time trying to construct a female territory within her husband's
prairie setting—the terrain of male activity. Redefining the environment
from a female perspective "signals women's appropriation of wilderness
as feminized space, the excess term which unsettles the boundaries of
male power."[45]

It frightens me Paul, just when I think I know you… [Paul turns away, about to leave.] Well, I need flowers. They're part of my heritage. We've always had flower gardens. Over here they don't even have fences—hedges… There's no history. I want my son to have a sense of his past. (91)

Paul, on the other hand, ridicules her desire for an English garden because he is threatened by what he imagines to be her British superiority. "Only the English would put their history behind a fence." (91) Diana equates Paul's inability to understand with the lack of Canadian history. "…You don't even know what it is…that sense of…of continuity with…everything that's gone before…" (91) Paul asserts that Kiev is his "history." Diana begins to realize how absurd Paul's statements are, as he has never been to Kiev. She then touches on the deeper implications: that Paul is isolating her from her past and refusing to grant her an equal position in his social domain.

…You know what I'm talking about…you brought me here and wiped out my past. Are you going to tell me you've stopped loving me now? (91)

Paul tries to justify his behaviour, telling Diana, "well, you knew what you were in for before you married me!" (91) There is a long pause, as Paul realizes how he has deceived her. Paul softens towards Diana, and for the first time acknowledges her fate. "I've led you a hell of a dance, haven't I?" (91)

The scene ends with Diana and Paul in each others' arms, but it is a shaky reconciliation as none of the problems have been resolved. Diana does not question the gender power structures which have led to her helpless condition and Paul's autocratic stature. She does not scrutinize her lack of power and exclusion from the public world as a manifestation of male domination of women. Instead of focusing on the real issue—her own powerlessness, Diana retreats into the myth of romantic love, thereby giving up the struggle for autonomy and access to the social arena.

Luce, also feeling stultified by the limitations of her husband, soon realizes that Canada is not the same as America. And surrounded by the "fish and fog" of the maritimes, the American dream is unobtainable. After spending seven years in Halifax with Chuck, she discovers she cannot rely on him to become a success. "I cannot wait for you any longer Chuck. I am more than thirty years old. Time is passing—too much time."(93) To obtain the American dream Luce sees she must go to Toronto, the most 'American' city in Canada. Luce comes to the ultimate realization that only by relinquishing the security of her life with Chuck will she unearth her true being.

> So this time I go. Maybe this time I do go off my head ...this
> time I go as far as I can. I find out what is inside me. (93)

Ruth and Diana, on the other hand, remain in their marriages, and continue to experience feelings of isolation and frustration. To emphasize the fragmented condition of Ruth and Diana's inner world, Hollingsworth shifts in and out of each woman's consciousness, breaking the barriers of time and space. In 1957 on New Year's Eve, both Ruth and Diana, in solitude, try to come to terms with their precarious identity in Canada. Ruth writes a letter to her parents in Scotland and attempts to put on a brave front—that Dave loves children and that people in Canada have "lots of money." But her letter reveals her adaptation as incomplete.

> Well, it's the end of another year, and I've a few minutes
> before I get on with Dave's tea. I wanted to write—you'll
> be wondering why I haven't written—well to tell you the
> truth, the sixth one's on the way—Dave's real pleased, he
> loves children. I'm sending a picture of us all, that's me in
> the back. (97)

The end of Ruth's letter unveils her deep-rooted loneliness and her longing to go home as she sits drinking alone.

> [Takes a drink.] Tell Angus to hurry up and come up on the races so he can send me a ticket to come home. I miss you...no. [Drinks.] Love from Ruthie. (97)

Diana, left alone while Paul is visiting his father in Saskatchewan, elucidates the private turmoil of her adjustment to Canadian life:

> ...There are times—there were times, when I'd look at the sky and wonder if it would be the same sky that they were seeing back home, or was it some other planet? It was so flat...and so cold in winter—the first year was the worst. The way you could hear the wolves and coyotes. I never told him...I thought I was on the edge of the world—the flatness under the snow. (99)

Diana recalls the terror and alienation evoked by the wilderness, so distant from the familiarity of English society. But she finds herself even more of a foreigner in her homeland. Diana is finally able to articulate her sense of insignificance caused by the suffocating isolation of her prairie environment. However, this awareness does not lead Diana toward a position of autonomy.

> ...Then when I went back home I couldn't sleep for the traffic noises...and we didn't even live near a main road. I was—funny how ashamed I still am of those old feelings—lonely. [Shivers, catches her arms around herself.] But this is my country now...I belong here. Paul...[Looks around, suddenly scared.] Paul, don't stay away. (99)

By accepting Canada as her home, Diana assimilates into her husband's life. Diana's prairie setting is an endorsement of Paul's world; thereby preventing her from achieving an individual perception of her own reality. Reminiscent of Mrs. Bentley in Ross's *As For Me and My House,* and Ruth in *Still Stands the House,* the wilderness mirrors Diana's own vulnerability, forcing her to turn to her husband for safety and protection. By accommodating herself to Paul's social domain Diana gives up her past identity and adopts his as her own.

Ruth's position as an exile is the most tragic. As shown, her situation as the victim is produced in part by the limitations of her social milieu, but more significantly, by her inexorable domestic world and the cruel indifference of her husband. Dave refuses to let her go to Scotland, claiming ostensibly that they don't have the money. Even when Ruth wins prize money in a contest and makes plans to take a trip home to visit her family, Dave tells her he has already spent the money on a car. "This way we can have an extra half hour in bed in the morning. I won't have to take the bus." (87) Ruth points out that she will still have to get up as usual for the children.

Ruth becomes increasingly marginalized and her status as an outcast intensifies as she must go out alone. She comes home drunk, only to find she is locked out.

> Come on out and hit me. They were singing Scottish songs...
> They asked us to come back next Friday—me and Molly
> McLaren. We danced...on the tables. We did so! Aye. [Giggles.] They don't really like us here, me and Molly. They
> don't like us, 'cos we're not Canadians. And I'll tell you
> something. [Giggles.] We don't like them either. [Sticks out
> her tongue childishly.] (102)

Like Diana, she associates her sense of displacement with the Canadian experience. They have no clear insight into what Canadian society might offer, just as they have no concrete knowledge of themselves as women, except what has been defined by their husbands. Contrary to Diana and Ruth, Luce's conviction that she can attain her own definition of Canada separates her most profoundly from the two other women.

Luce, on New Year's Eve, is broadcasting in Toronto after five years of living independently. Unlike that of Ruth and Diana, the inner consciousness of Luce is not revealed; instead she is shown as a public figure broadcasting on radio. It is not until several years later, in 1966, that Luce's destiny is further revealed. She runs into Chuck on Ste-Catherine Street in Montreal. She has just recorded an album and is currently rehearsing a cabaret show in Toronto. Chuck has married the girl who used to work in his father's restaurant and has two sons. He is in Montreal trying to perform at local hotels. Luce offers to help him get a contract at the Holiday Inn in Toronto, proving her success has been greater than his. "Maybe I can do something for you. Here. [Gives him her card.] Why don't you give me a call when you get into town." (101)

The last scene of the play sees the fusion of the three streams of female consciousness. The structure of the play synthesizes this amalgamation, as the last scene is a continuation of the first scene of the play which began in 1970, with Ruth, Dave, Diana and Paul gathered together in Niagara Falls. While the two couples eat their dinner, Luce sits at a table nearby, listening to Chuck play the piano. Although they are divorced, they are shown to be friends. Luce has just obtained the job for Chuck at the Holiday Inn in Toronto and he is performing his last show before going to Toronto.

The dinner conversation provides the external setting in which the two couples discuss their lives. On this superficial level Diana urges Paul to tell them how he has been "King Pin" in his bowling league, and then proceeds to tell Ruth and Dave, "It's been an enormously...full life." (103) Her tone suggests the inner uncertainty below the surface reality, and on a deeper level, the uncertainty of her own identity. Dave confronts Diana's ambivalence: "Full?" Diana is unable to elaborate, and realizing the insincerity of her remark, she motions to Paul to finish her fractured train of thought. Paul confirms what Diana is saying: "You're dead right," and then confidentially reveals the truth of their relationship to Ruth. "We hardly see each other."

Diana appears to have integrated into the prairie social setting. The farm is now fairly lucrative; she has become involved in various committees in an attempt to forge her own identity. Paul is shown to resent her involvement in all these activities, confiding in Ruth, "But you try living with someone who heads up just about every goddamned committee that's going!" (104)

The dialogue swings from superficial chit chat where they try to impress one another to the fragmented revelations of inner consciousness where intimate details of the hidden frustration in their lives is exposed. Paul and Ruth dance and Dave and Diana begin to unravel their lives on a more personal level. Dave confronts Diana about her life in Canada, hoping to get her to speculate on what her life might have been like if she had stayed in England. Through his probing, Dave reveals how he perceives her coming to Canada strictly in terms of the war, saying that she would not have come otherwise. Diana describes her reasons for coming beyond the external concerns of the war and touches upon the socio-political reasons for the three women's emigration. If she had stayed in England, she would have been trapped in a lifestyle dictated by her upper-class social milieu. "I'd've been married to some stuffy stockbroker probably." (105) There is a sense of irony as Diana articulates the all-encompassing power of patriarchy. She has merely exchanged one patriarchal system for another; escaping from one imprisonment only to find herself in another.

Dave's inquiry into Diana's inner world unites the inner consciousness of Diana and Ruth as his questions might just have been asked to his wife. "You don't think you'd'a been better off?" As he continues to question Diana, his resentment of British control over Canada multiplies. "How come you Brits always have to tell us what to do?" Although he articulates the Canadian sense of displacement due to British domination, he is unaware of the female sense of inadequacy induced by patriarchal control. Dave fails to see the connection between the "national dependence"[46] of Canada in the colonial tradition and women's historical dependence in patriarchy, for both are manifestations of the "exploited colony."[47]

The three immigrant women share the same female consciousness, but only on an unconscious level: consciously, they are unaware of their deep-seated feelings. Ruth asks Luce for her autograph and mentions that they all met during the war. Luce replies that she and Chuck also met during the war. Realizing that Luce is also a war bride, Ruth remarks, "Everything... changes doesn't it?" (108) Their conversation ends and Ruth goes back to her table. But on a deeper level they are connected more than they realize: as women and as foreigners who experienced homologous feelings of alienation in their struggle for integration into a hostile setting. Luce is the only one who breaks out of the patriarchal enclosure and is therefore a symbol of Ruth and Diana's unrealized female potential.

Diana continues to keep up appearances and talks about Paul's political activities. "Paul headed up our local campaign committee at the last election. We got to know Eugene Whelan personally, didn't we sweetie?" (108) But through their dinner conversation scattered portions of their private worlds emerge. When Paul questions why Ruth never went back to Scotland, she replies, "I was afraid I...I just might not've come back." Ruth reveals to Diana that the children want her to leave Dave. She then begins to reflect upon her Scottish roots and wonders if the pianist (Chuck) knows any old songs. Ruth's blatant honesty makes Diana uncomfortable, and she tries to keep the conversation light. "Talking of going home, the last time I was in the old country they seemed to think I was some kind of hillbilly." But Diana's remark unmasks her own extraneous loss of heritage, as she herself cannot go back. She has become a foreigner in her own country and is forced to embrace Canada as her place of refuge. But this inauguration into Canadian society is incomplete, just as integration within the boundaries of patriarchy is never absolute because it is a "sex-divided reality."[48] Both Ruth and Diana's assimilation into Canadian society personifies the relinquishment of their individuality within the patriarchal mold.

The death of Ruth's father symbolizes her broken ties with her past. However, her daughter Rita represents her unacknowledged female self and the link with her motherland of Scotland. As Rita has a university degree, she is equipped to determine the individuality Ruth was denied. Diana, on the other hand, feels no such bond with her son who wants to learn Ukrainian and identifies more with his father's background.

Diana and Ruth's reflections are interrupted by Dave's aggression as he begins to feel threatened by the women's intimacy.

> I'm sick of hearing you run it down. It's the best goddamned country in…You should be grateful to be here. All of you … [Shouts.] All of you. I fought for Canada. It's the greatest goddamned country in the world, so what's the matter with you all? You name one that's better. Scotland? Don't make me laugh. England? It's a joke. (109-110)

Again Dave's resentment towards Ruth mirrors his own Canadian sense of hostility towards British control. He does not realize that just as he feels inadequate in the face of colonial influence, Ruth feels without place in the face of patriarchal power.

Playwrights like John Coulter *(Riel)* and George Ryga *(The Ecstasy of Rita Joe* and *Indian)* describe imperial domination by drawing a parallel between Indian exploitation by the white man and Canadian control by British and American powers. Ryga's vision expresses the "lack of authentic language"[49] of the Cree Indians, and, on a national scale, the lack of an authentic language to articulate the distinctness of Canadian experience. However, Ryga's statements recognize only the Indian search for identity, overlooking the notion of gender as exemplifying the national search for identity.

The term "collective victim"[50] encompasses the recurring struggle for identity in the Canadian literary imagination. The 'collective victim' includes a "victimized country, a victimized minority group or a victimized individual."[51] The oppression of women as a literary symbol adds another dimension to the evolution of the Canadian consciousness. The female "question of being authentic,"[52] mirrors the national search for an "authentic language." The domination of Canada by British and American imperialism has impelled Canadians to seek national definitions "on our own terms."[53] The influence of these external interferences has made Canadians struggle against becoming "carbon copies"[54] of these powerful nations. Women playwrights like Margaret Hollingsworth stretch the boundaries of the dramatic imagination by expressing the need for an authentic female voice as part of the national literary search for identity.

As an expression of the lack of insight into female experience, Dave can only perceive his personal inadequacy in relation to colonial rule and national dependence. By undermining Ruth's heritage, he reveals the depth of his indifference towards her alienation from her past. Ruth gets up to sneak a drink from her bottle hidden in her purse, her alcoholism being symptomatic of her non-being and silent domestic misery. Dave prevents her from going off to drink alone and coaxes her to make a toast to Canada, which is an ironic way of toasting her subordination in Canadian society.

Both Ruth and Diana accept Dave's resentment without responding to his scorn for their homeland in an attempt to praise Canada. Nor do the women allow his open hostility towards colonial domination to provoke their own frustration in being controlled by the male disposition. Diana shows her conformity to patriarchal values by raising her glass and toasting, "To us, to all of us, and to Canada." (110)

Dave then perceives Ruth in connection with Canada. In the way he sees Canada as "the best goddamned country in the world," he now praises Ruth as having been "the best wife a man could have and I won't let any of you say any different." (110)

The final action of the play shows the two couples dancing while Luce and Chuck sing a duet. There is an ambiguous sense of unity as the couples overlook the deeper implications of Dave's outburst and the passive response of both Diana and Ruth. Ruth's inertia epitomizes her severe state of oppression, one that has destroyed her ability to free herself.

There is a suggestion of irony at the end of the play as the two couples dance together, suggesting that Ruth and Diana have kept their marriages going by the illusion of romantic love. Their self-deception signifies their inability to perceive reality through their own eyes. By escaping into a romantic fantasy they need not face the pain of bringing their dissatisfaction into the open. Luce, on the other hand, instead of living the romantic myth, is merely singing about it. As a symbol for the unattained female potential of Ruth and Diana, Luce has transcended the psychological boundaries that continue to confine their untapped resources.

NOTES

1. Howells, Coral Ann. *Private and Fictional Words: Canadian Women Novelists of the 70's and 80's*, London and New York: Methuen, 1987. p. 15.
2. Wallace, Robert and Zimmerman, Cynthia. eds. *The Work: Conversations with English-Canadian Playwrights*, Toronto: The Coach House Press, 1982, p. 93.
3. Moss, John George. *Patterns of Isolation in English Canadian Fiction*, Toronto: McClelland and Stewart, 1974, p. 13.
4. Ibid.
5. Ibid.
6. Ibid.
7. Howells. p. 2.
8. Millett, Kate. *Sexual Politics*, Garden City, N.Y.: Doubleday, 1970, p. 54.

9. Ibid. p. 26.
10. Ibid.
11. Atwood, Margaret. "Afterword," *The Journals of Susanna Moodie,* Toronto: Oxford University Press, 1970, p. 62.
12. Moss. p. 84.
13. Kreisel, Henry. "The Prairie: A State of Mind," *Contexts of Canadian Criticism,* ed. Eli Mandel, Chicago: University of Chicago Press, 1971, p. 257.
14. Frye, Northrop. *The Bush Garden,* Toronto: Anansi Press, 1971, p. 225.
15. Ibid.
16. Janeway, Elizabeth. *Man's World Woman's Place: A Study in Social Mythology,* New York: Morrow, 1971, p. 56.
17. Firestone, Shulamith. *The Dialectic of Sex,* New York: Morrow, 1970, p. 126.
18. Ibid. p. 166.
19. Trofimenkoff, Susan Mann. "Nationalism, Feminism and Canadian Intellectual History," *Canadian Literature,* 83 (Winter 1979) p. 16.
20. Ibid. p.11.
21. Frye. p. 239.
22. Ibid. p. 238.
23. Atwood, Margaret. *Survival,* Toronto: Anansi, 1972, p. 151.
24. Ibid. p. 157.
25. Ibid. *Survival,* p. 202.
26. Kreisel. p. 260.
27. Ibid. p. 261.
28. Atwood. *Survival,* p. 201.
29. Rich, Adrienne. *Of Woman Born,* New York: W.W. Norton and Company, Inc. 1976, p. 57.
30. Storrie, Kathleen. ed. *Women: Isolation and Bonding,* Toronto: Methuen, 1987, p. 4.
31. Ibid. p. 9.
32. Rich. p. 13.

33. Beauvoir, Simone de. *The Second Sex,* New York: A.A. Knopf Inc. 1953. Vintage Books Edition, 1974. p. 480.
34. Storrie. p. 1.
35. Ibid. p. 1.
36. Millett. p. 31.
37. Firestone. p. 161.
38. Moss. p. 84.
39. Ibid.
40. Ibid. p. 65.
41. Firestone p. 157.
42. Ibid. p. 167.
43. Moss. p. 54.

44. Stacey, Margaret and Marion Price. *Women, Power, and Politics,* London: Tavistock Publications, 1981, p. 7.
45. Howells. p. 18.
46. Boag, Veronica Strong. "Cousin Cinderella: A Guide to Historical Literature Pertaining to Canadian Women," in *Women in Canada,* Marylee Stephenson, ed. Don Mills, Ontario: General Publishing Co. Ltd. 1977, p. 246.
47. Atwood. *Survival,* p. 41.
48. Firestone. p. 169.
49. Watson, David. "An Interview with George Ryga," cited in *Canadian Drama and the Critics,* Conolly, L.W. ed. Vancouver: Talonbooks, 1987, p. 44.
50. Atwood. *Survival,* p. 36.
51. Ibid.
52. Firestone. p. 157
53. Watson. Quoting George Ryga, cited in *Canadian Drama and the Critics,* p. 44.
54. Ibid.

III

Islands

In *Islands*, as in *Ever Loving*, the quest for female consciousness finds its expression in the imagery of wilderness. The protagonist's anxiety, her fear of non-being, force her to confront and overcome the dangers inherent in the physical environment. But unlike *Ever Loving*, where wilderness is synonymous with the male world, the wilderness in *Islands* offers the opportunity for female self-actualization, unhampered by the constraints imposed by patriarchal urban society.

The wilderness in *Islands*, then, sets the stage on which Muriel projects her inner world. By confronting the uncertainty of coping alone on a secluded island in British Columbia, Muriel is able to reject the trappings of social conventions. This escape from established structures offers the route toward self-discovery and is highly prevalent in Canadian literature. Margaret Atwood's *Surfacing* and Ringwood's play *The Lodge*, for example, both deal with the theme of escape to the wilds as a means of self-revelation. The "northern utopia,"[1] the unspoilt wilderness, untainted by the corruption of 'southern' civilization, becomes the means of deliverance.

> ...the northern wilderness is a place where men and women
> in flight from what they feel are the decadent and sterile
> values of the 'South' may seek a heightened self-aware-

ness—perhaps even perceptions so transcendental as to be termed 'salvation.'[2]

In *Islands,* Hollingsworth expresses the retreat from civilization through Muriel's flight northward to a secluded island in British Columbia, abandoning the stifling values of her mother's conventional world.

The escape to the wilderness in order to live the pioneer life is traditionally associated with male experience, whereas the role of women alone in the wilderness has often been that of victim. "Traditionally women have survived on the frontier as either wives or prostitutes—and therefore as followers, certainly not as trail-blazers."[3] By fleeing from the corruption of civilization, Muriel repudiates the demands of patriarchal society, and finds the courage to define herself in a situation outside social roles and expectations. In *Ever Loving,* the prairie wilderness is part of Diana's entrapment within the patriarchal tradition, as is the "fish and fog" of Luce's confinement in Halifax with her husband, Chuck. In *Islands,* Hollingsworth expands her dramatic vision of the wilderness myth by associating the idea of female escape from patriarchal tradition with the potential for new definitions offered in a natural setting.

The play *Islands* is a continuation of the play *Alli Alli Oh,* in which the relationship between Muriel and Alli, a woman Muriel rescues from a mental institution, is explored. While *Alli Alli Oh* focuses on the domestic oppression which leads to Alli's fragmented state of consciousness, *Islands* deals with Muriel's attempt to rid herself of social obligations, which includes the demands of Alli. In *Alli Alli Oh,* Alli is shown to share in Muriel's search for identity, whereas in *Islands,* Muriel begins to reject Alli in an attempt to achieve her own autonomy.

The island emblemizes Muriel's attainment of a separate identity and her disconnection from the demands of others. By metaphorically representing the island as a sanctuary, Hollingsworth espouses Margaret Atwood's concept of "The Island."[4] This implies the "island-as-body, self-contained, a Body Politic, evolving organically, with a hierarchical structure…"[5] and is, in Atwood's view, the British symbol of refuge and security. To this Hollingsworth adds the Canadian myth of wilderness, implicit in which are the notions of escape and survival. Muriel's decision to live on the island symbolizes both the Canadian "spiritual survival"[6] metaphor, and the British metaphor of island as haven and stronghold. By interiorizing her struggle for survival against the external elements of the wilderness, Muriel takes on the responsibility for her own process of development and salvation.

The opening scene of the play shows Muriel absorbed at her drawing board where she designs experimental techniques for her farm. Through Muriel's efforts to be self-sufficient in organizing her new life, Hollingsworth suggests the correlation between the protagonist's building of her own farm and acquiring recognition of her own powers. Like the protagonist in *The Tomorrow Box,* by Anne Chislett, Muriel's farm gives her life meaning. On an individual level, in both plays, the women reject human relationships in an attempt to define their own selfhood in relation to the farm they manage.

The wilderness in *Islands* is an expression of female interior space which the protagonist tries to map out. On the secluded island, Muriel seeks to create a self-contained reality. Uncertain about her identity within society and her family, Muriel finds the untamed island a stimulating setting in which she can project her inner self.

In her social realm on the mainland of British Columbia, Muriel had no clear definition of self. In solitude on the island, Muriel is able to explore and penetrate her inner psyche without intrusion. Muriel's new understanding of self is expressed in the shaping of her external reality and the defining of her female sense of place.

> I looked around here…tried to take stock of the old place. I
> began to see…how…how unfocused I'd allowed myself to
> get. I'd started clearing a couple of spots, got a few head of
> stock, couple of hens, weatherproofed part of the barn, made

a half-assed attempt at rewiring. Nothing carried through.
I'd let myself get sloppy. [Waits for a response.] I took too
much notice of other people. (126-127)

Produced in 1977, *Islands* embodies the feminist quest for alternatives
to women's traditional position according to patriarchal doctrine. Muriel
exudes the feminist rejection of the stereotypical role of women, one that
"assigns domestic service and attendance upon infants to the female, the
rest of human achievement, interest, and ambition to the male."[7] Repre-
sentative of sex role stereotypes within conventional society is Rose,
Muriel's mother. When Rose comes to visit Muriel for the first time in five
years, she is a reminder of the conformity from which Muriel has tried to
escape.

ROSE: You can't build a house. [MURIEL continues to work.] Not
          on your own.
MURIEL: I'll get help. If I need it.
ROSE: Your grandfather built our house. It nearly killed him. Look
          at your hands. [Pause.] I'm not against hard work. I've
          worked hard all my life. [Points at the blueprint.]
          That's man's work. [Long pause. MURIEL works.] (122)

In the setting of the island, outside the boundaries of society, Muriel
attempts to rid herself of the limited role of women. This expression of a
gender-divided society has created what Michele Barrett sees as a "sexual
division of labour,"[8] whereby the duties of men and women are determined by the ideology of gender. Rose, working within the domestic realm
of the traditional female role, interprets her daughter's desire to live alone
and work the land as a deviation from that role.

The dialogue in the play shifts from the level of surface reality as Rose
talks about her new fiancé, Chuck, to the intimate probing of Muriel, who
confronts her mother's social world.

ROSE: Oh, he's used to farm people. He was in the bank for thirty-
           five years. He said they'd have folded up without the
           farmers.
MURIEL: Sure, they milked every goddamn farmer for miles around.
           (122)

Muriel sees her mother's relationship with Chuck as part of the corruption of society from which she has fled. Murial believes Chuck, as a banker, was instrumental in exploiting the farmers and destroying their connection with the land. To Muriel, Rose's reality is one that is disconnected from the natural world, thus threatening to devastate natural life.

MURIEL: [Points to a flower.] That's a protected species.
ROSE: I only took one or two. They're so pretty. They don't grow in
           Alberta, do they? I've never seen them.
MURIEL: If they did they'd have been wiped out years ago. [ROSE
           looks for something to do.] Why don't you pour
           yourself a drink? (123)

The violation of the natural environment is linked to the disruption of Muriel's private world of solitude on the island. By describing her life with Chuck, and their visit with his "married daughter" in Toronto, Rose attempts to revivify Muriel's acceptance of the traditional place of women in society. Muriel counterattacks by forcing her mother to question her own stereotypical notions of female behaviour she accepts as inviolable.

MURIEL: Did you know about the cockfights?
ROSE: He was a fine man.
MURIEL: On Wednesday nights. When you were at the Ladies'
           Auxiliary...
ROSE: On Wednesdays...I...

MURIEL: Well everyone else knew. They used to come to our place in droves. It was all very fast. Very hush-hush.

ROSE: I think I will make the chowder tonight. [ROSE brings a bucket in from the porch.] (124)

Rose is portrayed as the traditional mother who sacrifices her own individuality for the sake of the family. Her unquestioning acceptance of her role creates an illusion of harmony, concealing the truth behind a mask of assumed moral values.

In the natural setting of the wilderness, stimulated by the wild landscape far from the confines of established society, Rose begins to reflect upon her role as a mother and wife. She reveals to Muriel for the first time that she knew about the illicit activities of Muriel's father.

ROSE: I used to dread Wednesdays.

MURIEL: You knew?

ROSE: I lived with him. (124)

Both Muriel and Rose attain a new level of intimacy, by expressing feelings they previously concealed. Rose reveals the hypocrisies of her position as the peace-keeping wife and mother, and finally admits she knew about the cockfights and her husband's affairs. However, when she thinks of her relationship with Chuck, she quickly returns to her former orthodox approach. Afraid of the powerful feelings evoked by her confessions to Muriel, Rose tries to bring the level of discussion back to the boundaries of surface reality. "No. [Long pause. ROSE looks nervously at the door.] Don't you say a word about this to Chuck. Do you hear me?" (124) Rose seems most concerned that Chuck's expectations be upheld, again by concealing the truth, and clings tenaciously to the moral values Chuck represents. Rose's hypocrisy is apparent when she must keep an air of respectability by not sharing a bed with Chuck when he comes. "It wouldn't be suitable." (125) Nor does she find it suitable to share a bed with Muriel.

ROSE: Well...he might be... I don't want him to think there's
           anything funny—you and me—in your bed.
MURIEL: [Bursts out laughing.] You can't be serious!
ROSE: Well, he's bound to notice that you're...
MURIEL: [Cuts in.] I? I'm what?
ROSE: You're not married.
MURIEL: Does he judge women on their marital status? Sounds like a
           typical banker.
ROSE: Just a man that's all. He might not understand.
MURIEL: [Huffily.] Can't say I do either. (125)

Muriel's sense of betrayal indicates the ambivalent relationship between herself and her mother. She feels protective of her mother's helplessness, but at the same time blames her mother for being weak and
complacent.

MURIEL: [Looks up with sudden decision.] You know...You know...I
           used to think you needed me. I stuck around longer
           than I wanted to because...I thought he used you and
           you needed me as a buffer against him. And now I find
           out that even that was a sham—that you knew all the
           time. You probably even knew about his shenanigans
           with Maggie Butler. (125-126)

In response to Muriel's anger, Rose defends her position by saying: "If you
marry a wild man you take the consequences." (126) Jean Baker Miller
writes about the position of motherhood in patriarchy and its effect on
mother-daughter relationships:

Mothers have been deprived and devalued and conscripted
as agents of a system that diminished all women. Daughters
have felt the confusing repercussions of all of these forces.

Further, it is impossible to analyze the mother-daughter relationship without an analysis of the actions of the father, more accurately an analysis of the overall context which defines the family structure.[9]

The depiction of motherhood and patriarchy in the play also reflects Adrienne Rich's analysis of "motherhood as institution,"[10] whereby motherhood is an extension of male control which has "ghettoized and degraded female potentialities."[11] Rose exemplifies this institution of wife and motherhood by her internalization of gender stereotypes, what de Beauvoir calls "bad faith"[12] and Barrett calls "false consciousness."[13] Muriel tries to make her mother see that her father "hated women," (126) and reveals her resentment towards her father for fostering Rose's self-sacrificial approach. Muriel realizes her parents offered no guidance outside gender uniformity and finds she cannot identify with her mother in her search for individuality. Muriel is also angry for not being taken seriously as a woman.

MURIEL: I told you I'd make it alone. Well I have, haven't I? I ran a business—I got this place together and now I'm going to build the best goddamn house on the island. On my own. To my own design. (126)

Muriel's insistence on managing her own farm alone is a clear renunciation of the expectations of her parents. Muriel's father left the family farm to her brother, Ronnie, even though he was incompetent as a farmer and never wanted to work the land. Muriel, although she showed a natural talent for farming, was denied inheritance because she was a woman. Rose reaffirms her late husband's perception of farming as an 'unproper' vocation for women, and reminds Muriel of the importance of social interaction. "You can't isolate yourself. We all need other people." (126) But Muriel sees isolation as a form of protection.

MURIEL: Look mum—I'll try to explain. [Goes over and sits beside ROSE.] I don't mean to be hard. I just have to protect myself. I have to do things my way. Without interference from outside.

ROSE: No man is an island.

MURIEL: I'm a woman! (126)

Rose reveals that she does not perceive the quest for individuality as part of female experience.

Through her quest for identity, Muriel finds that even in the wilderness she can be stifled by the intrusion of others. Prior to her mother's visit, as depicted in *Alli Alli Oh*, Muriel had been living with Alli in a lesbian relationship, perceiving lesbianism as an escape from patriarchal domination. Miller expresses this concept of lesbianism as a diversion from gender power structures. "...lesbian women by their very existence challenge the fundamental structure of women's dependence on men."[14]

In her quest for an alternative to her limited upbringing, Muriel discovers that her lesbian relationship with Alli is not a solution to the traditional female role, as Muriel finds that even with Alli her individuality is threatened. The fact that Muriel cannot tell Rose about her lesbian affair shows Muriel is still controlled by the values and expectations of her mother's world. Muriel's involvement with Alli represents the exploration of a love relationship outside the conventional realm defined by her mother—an involvement she had hoped would not restrict her human growth. On this subject, the collective writings of Radicalesbian claim,

[The lesbian] is the woman who, often beginning at an extremely early age, acts in accordance with her inner compulsion to be a more complete and freer human being than her society cares to allow her...She may not be fully conscious of the political implications of what for her began as personal necessity, but on some level she has not been able to accept the limitations and oppression laid on her by the most basic role of her society—the female role.[15]

Muriel's venture beyond the borders of prevailing sexual behaviour shows an interesting parallel with her exploration of new, revolutionary farming methods, particularly "hydroponics," by which plants are grown without soil, itself symbolic of Muriel's search for self-sufficiency. For just as Muriel's experiments expand the limits of traditional farming, her lesbian encounter is also a deliberate departure from the traditional male-female relationship, as living with Alli excludes the role of wife and motherhood. But Muriel is shown to reject lesbianism as a substitute for male-female relationships and instead chooses solitude.

> ...I began to see it all in perspective. Not just my life but all the rest. On this island, in Canada, in every developed country. We're all being forced into living alone—being alone—don't you see? Relationships don't make sense any more. (127)

Rather than any kind of relationship Muriel seeks satisfaction in a self-chosen project, and turns her energy towards creativity in order to achieve fulfillment.

> I'm going to work up a business on my own. On a really big scale. See here—here's the outline [Points to wall chart.] I've got it all planned. I should have the foundations of the house in by June. I figure that by December I'll be clear enough to make a start on the greenhouses. If I get a good run at it... not too much rain. (127)

Experimenting with her environment by producing plants through hydroponics can be seen as Muriel's attempt to gain control over her environment, thus shaping it to her own design. Muriel's plan to use science and technology to make plants grow without soil is a manipulation of the natural world, one that changes the life process. To Muriel, this becomes the creative ordering of her physical environment. As Miller points out the connection between personal change and the transformation of reality:

> For women to act and react out of their own beings is to fly in the face of their appointed definition and their prescribed way of living. To move toward authenticity, then, also involves creation, in an immediate and pressing personal way. The whole fabric of one's life begins to change, and one sees it in a new light.[16]

Rose, on the other hand, does not see Muriel's activities in terms of individual growth, but as unnatural. She reminds Muriel of the traditional perception of women in relation to men.

ROSE: I'll bet there's a dozen good men who'd come here on an hour's notice if you'd only give them half a chance.

MURIEL: It'll run itself. No need for men.

ROSE: What if something happened to you? You could lie in a ditch for days—

MURIEL: Nothing's gonna to happen to me— (127)

In perceiving women as helpless, Rose attempts to undermine Muriel's efforts to obtain control over her own life. Hilary Lips writes about cultural images of female weakness and the exclusion of positive images of female strength and power.

...the accepted imagery of power and the accepted imagery
of femininity in this society are totally incompatible and
mutually exclusive. "Proper" feminine images are filled with
powerlessness and weakness, and those feminine images
which do incorporate power are portrayed as evil and
frightening...[17]

Muriel's desire for self-empowerment includes the reassessing of social
values and political systems. Her disillusionment with her family and the
stereotyped position of women in society leads Muriel to reflect on the
breakdown of all social institutions.

MURIEL: You can't have a political system that's built up on single
           isolated entities. Politicians depend on mass sentiment.
           You know, if they were really interested in our
           well-being they'd be educating us to live alone. But
           they daren't. They'd rather see us freak out. It's
           unacceptable isn't it? A woman on her own—making it
           without help from the system. Do they still make jokes
           about spinsters back home? (128)

Muriel shows that her rejection of habitual female behaviour includes
the abandonment of all social ideologies that limit individual potential.
Through her separation from society, she becomes aware that the struggle
for selfhood in mainstream society is stunted by social indoctrination. This is
a restatement of the feminist claim that patriarchy is a socio-political "institution" controlling all aspects of life and "every avenue of power within the
society..."[18] Rose is shown to have internalized the very conventions her
daughter is attacking when she voices the traditional role of women as well
as her evasion of her own autonomy. "I guess I need a man of my own." (128)

Rose's intrusion in Muriel's life signifies the difficulty Muriel has in
shaking the restrictions of her social realm. By announcing that she would

like to come and live on the island with Chuck, Rose and the patriarchal society she represents, become a threat to Muriel's private world. "Ronnie and the kids can come out here in the winter—he likes to get away in winter. We can all be together." (129) Both Muriel's inner world and her external world, the island, are threatened by the invasion of society and its expectations from which she has tried to escape. She tries to discourage her mother from moving to the island. "Property prices are astronomical. Water front—do you know what you're looking at?" (129) Muriel fears being drawn into her mother's stifling world, and as an affirmation of Muriel's fears, Rose reminds her of her deviation from her expected role according to social norms. "Your father always used to say that the blood got mixed up. You were the oldest and you should have been the boy, then it would all have worked out." (130) Stacey and Price write about the uneasiness caused by women breaking the gender mold.

> Notions of the 'proper place' and 'proper behaviour' are deeply ingrained and emotionally loaded, such that acute discomfort is felt when the norms are violated. For the actors concerned, the norms have come to appear as 'natural', as part of an externally given order without which there could only be chaos. Thus deviants must be put down and the order maintained.[19]

Muriel's anger mounts as she recalls how her mother upheld gender roles and acquiesced to her husband's decision to force Ronnie into farming and Muriel into studying for an arts degree. "When it came to the crunch, you went along with him." (130) Rose reverberates the perception of woman's place inside the patriarchal model. "I didn't want you to ruin your life. I wanted you to grow into a...a woman."... "Yes. A woman. I wanted you to have children." (130)

By expecting Muriel to fulfill the traditional female role, Rose, as a mother, is shown to be instrumental in perpetuating the dichotomy of gender identity. Stacey and Price believe women, by not trying to change the accepted norms, have been "architects of the reproduction of their own oppression."[20]

As young women of the 1970's, like Muriel, struggle to liberate themselves from their mothers, whom they see as having "taught a compromise and self-hatred,"[21] Rich points out that it is easier "to hate and reject a mother outright than to see beyond her to the forces acting upon her."[22] Thus Rose's limited perception of her daughter's potential stems from her own lack of opportunity and unfulfillment under patriarchy.

Alli, who arrives without warning, is the antithesis of the conforming woman. Mentally ill and bisexual, she lives on the periphery of conventional society. Nevertheless, Alli tries to identify with Rose, telling Rose that she herself is a mother and was married for eighteen years. Alli discusses her children with Rose: "Yes. Mine are called Denny and Christine. Christine's just had her seventeenth birthday. She's an Aries." (132) Alli eventually turns the level of reality away from trivialities towards the darker world of psychological fragmentation. By telling Rose about her experience in "the nut house," (133) Alli draws Rose into an unknown world. Her presence is shown to confront and disrupt Rose's established values. Where Rose sees the need to conceal and pretend in order to keep the harmony, Alli is overtly direct in her emotional and psychological expression.

ALLI: They said I should express whatever I have on my mind. They said that most sickness is caused by repressing one's natural feelings. [To Rose.] Do you agree with that?

ROSE: I'm not an expert in that sort of— (133)

Rose is the voice of the conventional woman who stifles the truth for the sake of appearances. By contrast, Alli is portrayed as mentally ill, thus allowing her to depart from society's customary perception of women. As she is also a lesbian, Alli defies the traditional view of female sexuality, and is seen as a threat to the moral fibre of her community. Alli's husband, who is demanding legal custody of their children, judges her to be an unfit mother. Muriel, on the other hand, does not believe that Alli is mentally ill, and explains Alli's repetition of phrases as a mantra, telling Rose, "I always thought of it as meditating." (134) While Muriel tries to justify Alli's behaviour to Rose, Alli asserts that she has been "cured" and adds, "I really don't have to talk to myself." (134)

Alli is constantly exposing and verbalizing what is hidden, including Muriel's inner feelings. "You're not very pleased about the bank teller, are you?" (p.134) Alli provokes both Rose and Muriel into disclosing intense emotions, using her mental instability as a shield against the reproach of others. Alli also enjoys the power she has over Muriel, knowing she dreads her mother finding out about their affair.

ALLI: Oh? [Laughs, to MURIEL.] Have you told her?

MURIEL: There's nothing to tell.

ALLI: You used to think there was. Don't you remember…? [Sings.] 'If she could see us now…' [Looks at MURIEL's frightened face.] No? [Takes a breath, turns to ROSE.] The hospital was on the mainland. A long way away.

ROSE: And now you're better.

MURIEL: Alli, look—

ALLI: Yes. Better.

MURIEL: For heaven's sake put your bag down. [Gets glasses and a bottle.] (135)

While Muriel and Rose camouflage their real feelings under a shroud of platitudes, Alli plunges into the cavities of her own guilt and inadequacy, confessing, "I can tell that you're a very good mother. [Pause. ROSE and MURIEL exchange looks.] I wasn't. I was a lousy mother. Terrible. Terrible." (135) Rose seems to remind Alli of her failure as a traditional mother and wife. The play suggests that Alli's mental disintegration is in part an escape from social responsibilities. By being mentally ill, she has a socially defined role, one that makes her failure as a wife and mother more acceptable. Although Alli perceives Rose as the ideal mother, she does not realize that Rose herself feels she has failed as a mother because of the way Muriel has turned out.

Both Rose and Alli epitomize different extremes: Rose denies her individuality in order to gain social acceptance; Alli rejects her role as mother and wife, as well as the prevailing feminine characteristics. Rose embodies the complete acceptance of convention and Alli exemplifies the total rejection of it. Where Rose is passive and inscrutable, Alli is aggressive and often cruel in her honesty. Alli ridicules Rose's need for romantic love when she notices the flowers Rose picked for Chuck, whom Alli calls her "financé."

ALLI: Oh. They're for the financé. [To ROSE.] You know you're lucky
           to get a second go. At your age.
MURIEL: Alli, that's obnoxious!
ROSE: No it's not. [Comes up to ALLI, speaks simply.] Yes, you're
           quite right. I do consider myself lucky. I'm a lucky
           woman. (136)

By calling Chuck Rose's "financé," Alli alludes to the economic and financial power of men in patriarchy, power women like Rose have historically depended upon.

Muriel is caught between the two extremes: surrendering to conventional ubiquity, as Rose does; or, like Alli, forsaking entirely the norms of society. Muriel's task is to find her own identity through the confrontation of both extremes. Although Muriel rejects her mother's position, Muriel shares her dislike of Alli's insensitive probing and disruption of social order; her destructive honesty. "You haven't changed a bit have you? You're a wrecker, Alli. A wrecker." (139) Now Muriel begins to break the

boundaries of polite behaviour, demonstrating her true feelings under-
neath. Alli replies, "You can't wreck what's already..." But Alli does not
finish her sentence, and instead returns to mundane reality, watching Rose
make tea. "I don't think the water was boiling." Like Muriel, Rose begins to
express underlying feelings of anger towards Alli and tells her to leave.
"You're upsetting my daughter." (139) Alli in turn shows her own hostility
towards Muriel for being unemotional and always "in control."

ALLI: Upsetting your daughter? Your daughter's calm. Made of steel,
your daughter. She's got a smile like a steel trap. Always
damn well in control. Everything under control. (139)

Alli begins to tell Rose and Muriel what happened to her after she left
the island. At this point both Rose and Muriel are drawn into Alli's inner
world. Muriel is shocked when she hears that Alli lived on the disreputable
Hastings Street and worked as a chambermaid. Alli tries to evoke feelings
of guilt in Muriel as she describes the humiliation and cruelty she en-
countered in the mental hospital. "They put a rubber gag in your mouth.
Your whole body...turns to water." (140) Muriel forgets her anger towards
Alli and together they cling to one another. At this point Rose is forced to
acknowledge the fact of her daughter's lesbian affair. The veil of decorum
is discarded, and Muriel reveals what she had been desperately trying to
conceal. At first Muriel blames her mother for interfering in her life,
claiming that if she had not come to visit, she would not have found out.
However, Muriel finally refuses to succumb to her mother's hypocrisy, and
reveals the truth.

MURIEL: Alli—[MURIEL puts her arms around ALLI, anguished.
They embrace and cling to each other. To ROSE.] Don't
stare. Don't stare at us. [ROSE gets up.] If you hadn't
come here...you can't go on keeping things quiet.

ROSE: Why not? Tell me why not?

MURIEL: It isn't honest, that's why.

ROSE: Honesty! (140)

But Rose, who wants to keep all experience within the confines of respectability, evades both honesty and self-knowledge. She would rather eschew authenticity than accept unpleasant truths. In contrast, Muriel realizes that honesty is crucial in achieving a definition of self, but like her mother, she has also been concealing hidden truths, as Rose points out: "All that talk about being on your own. It wasn't anything to do with it." (140) Muriel expresses her own concealed feelings of failure for not being the kind of woman her mother expected her to be. "Tell me I'm a freak then. Unnatural..." (140) Muriel feels caught between the two women and what they represent. She runs outside, unable to go to either of them.

Alli and Rose are left to talk alone, and Rose is brought further into Alli's world of psychological flux. Alli makes Rose deal with a side of female experience she has never acknowledged before. Alli describes her inner psyche, her intimate feelings. She tells Rose how her personal life was probed by the doctors in the hospital, and how she had been labeled a paranoid schizophrenic. "'What about your husband?' Cold storage. 'Were you on good terms—socially?' Cold storage. 'Sexually?' Cold storage." (141) Alli sees beyond the doctor's questions, for what the doctor really wanted to know was why she lost her mind. But Alli insists she is not crazy. "I didn't lose my mind—I just put it away for a while. In cold storage." (141) By putting her mind away in 'cold storage', Alli has taken on the role of mental illness as an alternative to her social position as housewife and mother.

After being released from the hospital, Alli wandered aimlessly around Hastings Street and found communion with an alcoholic native woman. Alli begins to draw Rose into her imagination through her sensitive description of the Indian woman.

> She had a bottle tucked between her breasts, under her
> blouse, with the neck sticking out...and she kept stroking it

as if it were a baby, or...or a lover. [She makes a stroking motion, turns away from the door and leans forward, as if watching.] She's very thin. [Faster.] Suddenly one of the guys leans across and pulls the bottle out—but he doesn't make it. She's awake in a second and she grabs the bottle and brings it down on his fingers. It smashes against the table. Blood and rye and no more smell of herring. And he yells, 'You know what you are? You're a man with a cunt. A man with a frigging cunt.' She doesn't say a word. Just listens. [Pause.] They leave. I lean across. I want her to listen to me you see. I want her to listen—but I've forgotten how to make her hear. She starts to eat the fish. Very delicately, dainty little piles, fish on one side, bones on the other. No fuss. [Pause.] I wanted to touch her, I wanted to feel what it was like to be that bottle, to come out of cold storage. She was so much herself. Like Muriel. (142)

In Canadian writing, the Indian has become a symbol of "the ultimate victim of social oppression and deprivation."[23] Like the Indian woman in George Ryga's *The Ecstasy of Rita Joe,* Ringwood's *Lament for Harmonica* and *The Stranger,* the Indian woman Alli describes is shown to struggle against her male oppressors. Alli identifies with the Indian woman because she possesses individuality and dignity in the face of despair. But at the same time Alli is baffled by the realization that the Indian woman must have stolen her wallet and eternity ring, which she finds are missing when she leaves the café. She goes back to look for them and finds the Indian woman has disappeared. Alli's search for the ring suggests her loss of eternal marital happiness, symbolized by the eternity ring. When the police come Alli says she is "looking for eternity," (143) connecting her quest for the ring with her individual search for integration and meaning.

It is at this point that Alli is thought to be insane and taken away to the hospital. The hospital officials demand an address before they agree to release her. "I told them I lived on an island. On a farm on an island, with a woman." (143) In Alli's state of instability, the island is her place of refuge from society and its corruption. As with Muriel, the island for Alli is a place to escape the expectations of others and offers her the harmony she seeks, what Mitcham sees as "the unmaterialistic regenerative potential"[24] of the wilderness.

Rose is unsure how to respond to Alli's display of inner feelings and emotional turmoil. When Alli tells her there are questions walking "all over town," (143) Rose tries to bring the statement into the context of light conversation. "I don't know the town. I only came to the coast once before." (143) Then Alli attempts to force Rose into a frank reaction, asking her how it feels, "knowing your daughter's a dyke." (143) Rose finally admits her true feelings: "You disgust me." (144) Alli replies eagerly, "Do I? Do I really?" (144) Alli has achieved the emotional reaction from Rose she had been waiting for, she has succeeded in breaking Rose's polite facade. After admitting her real feelings, Rose immediately feels sorry for what she said, realizing that Alli "can't help it." (144) By saying Alli "can't help it," Rose displays how she associates lesbianism with mental sickness and abnormality. Consequently, she is able to pity Alli and perceive her behaviour as less threatening.

Although their opposing realities clash with one another, Rose and Alli are forced into each other's inner worlds. Both must accept the different levels of female experience the other represents. Rose is made to acknowledge Alli's rejection of conventional values, and Alli is confronted with Rose's position within the patriarchal model. Rose begins to confide in Alli and expresses her feeling of failure as a 'good' mother.

ROSE: [Suddenly.] Is Muriel sick?
ALLI: Sick? You mean like me?
ROSE: Well—what did I do? Where did I go wrong?" (144)

Rose's sense of guilt stems from the heavy demands placed upon her as a mother. Within her socially defined role as a mother, Rose feels responsible for her daughter becoming "a woman," which means being married and having children. As Rich observes, "under the institution of motherhood, the mother is the first to blame if theory proves unworkable in practice, or if anything whatsoever goes wrong."[25]

Rose realizes Alli is unable to help her, as Alli herself has rejected her position as wife and mother. Alli can only respond, "You're so serious. Like Muriel." (144) At this point Rose wishes that Alli would go away, so that she can go back to her daily reality. Alli's repeated denial of Rose's social values has made her want to cling to those values even more. Rose also wants Alli out of her daughter's life and offers her money to go away, telling her to hide it from Muriel. Alli confronts Rose's need to keep things hidden. "You're always covering up after everybody. Like a cat—you give it something it doesn't like and it tries to cover it up. That's why I hate cats." (144) Alli then throws the money on the floor.

At this stage Chuck calls, rescuing Rose from this threatening and chaotic setting, bringing her back to her familiar world. Rose wants to keep Chuck separate from all this, as he symbolizes Rose's sense of security within the old patriarchal tradition, where Rose's position as a woman is clearly defined. Within the confines of her respectable social framework, Rose has found a limited kind of order and integration: an integration, however, that excludes the search for individuality outside the dictates of assigned roles. Thus Rose's inner world, the exploration of her inner female consciousness, is left untouched. Alli threatens this security when she suggests meeting Chuck.

ALLI: Shall we shake him up?
ROSE: No! You? Yes, you would, wouldn't you?
ALLI: He's not used to honesty?
ROSE: I don't know. (145)

However, Alli agrees to stay out of their way. Rose herself has decided to stay with Chuck in the lodge and come to visit Muriel during the day. Both

Rose and Alli leave for the mainland. As Alli prepares to leave, she picks up the money Rose gave her and puts it in her pocket.

There is a sense that Rose and Muriel have neither reconciled, nor become closer as mother and daughter. They are shown to "embrace briefly," (146) suggesting the affection they have for one another is marred by the continuing strain in their relationship. Muriel and Alli, on the other hand, are shown to "throw their arms around each other," expressing their deeper caring for one another.

Muriel finds herself alone again. She places the quilt made by Alli on the bed and sits on it, as if contemplating her involvement with Alli. Muriel then gets up from the bed and returns to her desk, choosing to focus her attention on the development of her farm. She must continue her search for self identity in the light of her newly defined relationship with both her mother and Alli. Rose and her conventional world, and Alli and her disordered world, have both disrupted Muriel's search for self-definition. Her relationship with Alli and Rose is still tenuous, as is her connection with the wilderness in which she must struggle to construct her own sense of place. What remains constant is Muriel's relation to the farm and the satisfaction her work brings when she is liberated from the demands of others. The last image focuses on Muriel alone, a common technique in women's plays, like Kelly Rebar's *Checkin' Out*, where the final frame of the heroine alone reflects her autonomy and self-actualization.

In both *Islands* and *Ever Loving*, Hollingsworth's exploration of female identity concerns the female characters' relation to their physical environment. In *Ever Loving*, the regional settings of Hamilton, Lethbridge and Halifax become mirror images of the three women's psychological and social entrapment within patriarchal marriages. In *Islands*, Hollingsworth is shown to transform the protagonist's relation to her physical environment. Whereas the physical landscape in *Ever Loving* reflects female oppression, the natural world in *Islands* is a projection of female creative potential. Thus Muriel's place in the wilderness is connected with her search for individuality and the liberation from the patriarchal mold.

Where Diana finds the prairie landscape an extension of her husband's power which subdues her, Muriel finds the secluded island an escape from the limitations of social expectations.

Both plays expound the 1970s feminist claim that the domestic position of women under patriarchy is oppressive to women. Both Luce in *Ever Loving* and Muriel in *Islands* refuse marriage and motherhood out of fear of losing their autonomy. Like Luce, Muriel is shown to break away from a restrictive social realm, but unlike Luce who seeks identity in an urban setting, Muriel withdraws from the urban, public world to the seclusion of nature. By becoming a farmer, a traditionally male vocation, Muriel's separation from urban mainstream society offers her power over her environment rather than isolation. However, Muriel's independence is not without a price. By protecting herself from the demands of others, Muriel chooses the safety of solitude and in the process limits the potential for self-enrichment through human companionship.

NOTES

1. Mithcham, Allison. *The Northern Imagination: A Study of Northern Canadian Literature,* Moonbeam, Ontario: Penumbra Press, 1983, p. 21.
2. Ibid. p. 17.
3. Ibid. p. 96.
4. Atwood. *Survival.* p. 32.
5. Ibid.
6. Ibid. p. 33.
7. Millett. p. 26.
8. Barrett, Michele. "Ideology and the Cultural Production of Gender," *Feminist Criticism and Social Change : Sex, Class, and Race in Literature and Culture,* eds. Judith Newton and Deborah Rosenfelt, New York and London: Methuen, 1985, p. 74.
9. Miller, Jean Baker. *Toward a New Psychology of Women,* Boston: Beacon Press, 1976, pp. 139-140.
10. Rich. p. 13.
11. Ibid.
12. de Beauvoir. p. 275.

13. Barrett. p. 82.
14. Miller. p. 138.
15. Radicalesbians. "The Woman-Identified Woman," in *Radical Feminism*, ed. Anne Koedt, New York: Quadrangle Books, 1970, p. 240.
16. Miller. pp. 113-114.
17. Lips, Hilary M. "Women and Power: Psychology's Search for New Directions," *Atlantis*, 5, no.1, (Fall 1979) p. 7.
18. Millett. p. 25.
19. Stacey and Price. p. 8.
20. Ibid. p. 10.
21. Rich. p. 235.
22. Ibid.
23. Atwood. *Survival*, p. 97.
24. Mitcham. p. 11.
25. Rich. p. 222.

IV

The Twisted Loaf

Aviva Ravel's play, *The Twisted Loaf,* like Hollingsworth's *Ever Loving,*
examines the 'immigrant exile' concept in conjunction with the female
search for identity and place. Ravel explores the sense of estrangement and
the concomitant quest for self-affirmation experienced by Bessie, a Russian-Jewish immigrant, in the foreign setting of Montreal. Like Ruth,
Diana and Luce in *Ever Loving,* Bessie's sense of dislocation and mar-
ginalization as an immigrant is magnified by her position as a woman. But
unlike the women in *Ever Loving,* Bessie is further sequestered from
mainstream society because she is Jewish.

A Jewish Montrealer herself, Ravel, like playwright Ted Allen and
novelist Mordecai Richler, probes the bewildering experience of at-
tempting to preserve exogenous cultural traditions, whilst concurrently
grappling with the fluctuating uncertainties of a new and unfamiliar
country. Elaine Newton perceives Canadian Jewish writing as a "sub-
genre of literature,"[1] one that epitomizes the immigrant pursuit of identity in association with the Canadian yearning for national definition.
Canadian Jewish writing represents the "symbolic importance of the
dualistic Jewish experience in a nation which is itself adolescent and
identity-seeking."[2]

The Twisted Loaf, published in 1970, exemplifies both the immigrant
search for identity and the female search for recognition in the burgeoning

women's movement. Bessie, by striving to achieve an integral feeling of belonging, attempts to adjust to North American values and customs which are completely at variance with those of her native Russian village. Unlike Luce and Diana in *Ever Loving,* she is not favoured by her social background, nor does she have the advantage of coming from an English-speaking country as do Ruth and Diana. Bessie, as a Jewish immigrant, has the additional barrier of adapting to an environment with a foreign language, religion, and culture. Seeking refuge in the Jewish ghetto, she acquires a sense of place, but in the process she becomes marginalized from the mainstream of Canadian society.

Dying in a hospital bed, Bessie, now 65, reflects upon her life as a young woman trying to forge a new life in a foreign country. The play opens with Bessie's recollections of her life in Russian society before she is sent to Canada. Even in her own country she is without place, for, as Jews, her family is disbarred from Russian society by anti-semitism. Unable to pay their rent, Bessie's family is forced into ruin and must sell all they possess, sending their young daughter, Bessie, alone to live with her uncle in Montreal.

The family's sense of loss is echoed by the auctioneer who sells their treasured candlesticks for profit. In the family's moment of despair, it is Bessie's mother who has the strength to find a way out of the misery and plan for a better future.

DAUGHTER: Where will we go tonight?
MOTHER:	To the auntie, and then, maybe a ticket to America.
FATHER:	Who will send us a ticket, who?
MOTHER:	My uncle. He's a good man.
FATHER:	May I rot in my grave before I take charity!
MOTHER:	We have no choice, papa. First we'll send Bessie and then, God willing, we'll go…
FATHER:	(Going off) The pogrom will get us first! (7)

Bessie returns to the present with the nightmare of the past fresh in her imagination, and the realization that she has created a better world for her own children. "Thank God I protected my children from that...ah my poor father." (7) Bessie's husband, Alex, comes to visit her in the hospital and their dialogue reveals fragments of their social world. Both Bessie and Alex are disappointed about the marriages of their two daughters, Judy and Annie, and by the life of their single daughter, Sheila. When Alex leaves the room, the focus shifts from surface reality to Bessie's inner reflections on the futility of her life-long struggle to achieve success for her daughters, when death only comes in the end. "Amount to something. In the end it all amounts to the same thing." (8-9)

Through her solitary contemplations about the hardships of her life, Bessie attempts to come to terms with herself and to reach self-definition. The stylistic device of creating two characters that represent Bessie's young and old self allows for the interaction between Bessie's inner consciousness and her external self, between the past and the present. The young energetic Bessie tells the old tired Bessie that she must return to her sewing, to support the family, to which Old Bessie replies, "I can't work no more." (9) Young Bessie says she can go on without her, and that she must continue buying food and clothes for the three children. "I have to get the work out. Annie and Sheila need shoes, and there's the grocery bill. Gottenu give me strength." (9) Bessie takes on the persona of her younger consciousness who is at home with her children, sewing to earn a living for the family when her husband is laid off from the clothing factory. It is Young Bessie who must provide the economic security and emotional strength to keep the family from poverty. But as a traditional woman, she is confined to working within the home, and borrows money from her uncle to start a home sewing-business, employing six girls.

Although Young Bessie becomes the generating force behind the income which supports the whole family, Alex is her link with the exterior world. "I'll manage everything. You'll just go to the manufacturers and get the work." (9) Using her uncle's position in the business world and her husband's access to the public world, she engineers a way to bring the labour market into her own home. Adrienne Rich discusses the enormous responsibilities undertaken by the early Jewish woman immigrant.

> Jewish women of the shtetl and ghetto and of the early immigrant period supported their Talmud-studying men, raised children, ran the family business, trafficked with the hostile gentile world, and in every practical and active way made possible the economic and cultural survival of the Jews.[3]

Young Bessie's will to overcome all obstacles pivots around the well-being of her three daughters, as well as a desire to offer hope and emotional support to her husband. "It's going to be good again. I want to live to see them well off. That's all I care." (9)

The focus of the play shifts forward to the present when her daughters meet to visit their mother in the hospital. Sheila reveals her hostility to her family and remembers her upbringing with bitterness.

SHEILA: You know what I learned at home? To hate. Everything and everybody. Especially little Judy princess. (Smiles) Remember I tied her to a post and forced her to eat worms? And I cut off her curly locks...served mama right for calling her "Shirley Temple." And once I set a match to her crib and she almost burned...gee I was a rotten kid. Mama was so good to her and you know how she paid her back—by marrying a 'goy'. Mama never got over it. (11)

By focusing on Judy's marriage outside the Jewish faith, Judy's failure appears greater than her own, for Judy's "defection" threatens the continuation of Jewish tradition. But as Sheila is unmarried, she too spurns Jewish convention in which marriage and family play an essential role.

The importance of the Jewish figure's cultural past is pivotal to the Canadian Jewish imagination. Richler's novel, *The Apprenticeship of Duddy Kravitz*, and Ted Allan's play, *Lies My Father Told Me*, show that success achieved at the expense of cultural and historical identity is illusory.

> The Jew in Canadian fiction is similarly a perennial exile for whom assimilation is tantamount to annihilation, and who thus remains an immigrant in an alien land, struggling through generations of change to maintain some semblance of the past in his present life.[4]

Although influenced by their background, Bessie's three daughters have acquired Canadian values through their attempt to integrate into society. By marrying a wealthy business man, Judy fulfills her mother's dream, but in the process repudiates her Jewish tradition as her children become Catholic like their father. Annie must support her family while her husband finishes his law degree; Sheila renounces her parents' expectations by living the unconventional life of a struggling writer and seeking solace in psychoanalysis. Like Alli in *Islands,* Sheila, by scrutinizing unpleasant truths, forces others to remove the shroud from their buried feelings.

SHEILA: Whatsamatter? The princess can't take it? Let's soften the blow then. Let's tell it to her slowly. Ma—ma...is...pass—ing...away.

ANNIE: Look Judy, it's like this. She won't get better, and the doctor wants to perform another operation.

JUDY: (Pale) Then she has got..oh, my God...

SHEILA: (Enjoys Judy's pain) Whose God do you think she's talking to, ours or Arthur's?

ANNIE: For godsake, Sheila, shut up!
JUDY: You're disgusting!
ANNIE: That was a rotten thing to say!
SHEILA: (Pauses and smiles) That's how it is. Everyone's always
            picking on me. (12)

But dissension and bitterness turn to concern as the sisters remember the traditional expectations of their mother. Their sense of failure is paramount when Annie tells Sheila to pretend she is successful. "Tell her...(Pause)...that your novel will be published. That you're going to be rich and famous!..." (12) As they prepare themselves to meet their mother, the focus of the play shifts to the younger consciousness of Bessie on the night she accepts Alex's proposal. In a foreign country, separate from her family, Bessie sees marriage as a way of finding security and social acceptance.

YOUNG BESSIE: My uncle says I shouldn't marry you.
YOUNG ALEX: Maybe he's right. I can't promise you
                'goldene glicken', just that I'll always love you.
YOUNG BESSIE: If I was in the old country my mother would choose
                me a husband. Here it's different.
YOUNG ALEX: You're beautiful, Bessie.
YOUNG BESSIE: A girl has to have a family, a home... (13)

Severed from a tradition in which her mother would choose her husband, Bessie must now make her own choices in a setting with opposing values and customs. However, what Bessie clings to is the belief that women need a husband for economic security. Like the women immigrants in *Ever Loving,* Bessie's acceptance of her role within the traditions of patriarchy is unquestioned. Even in the New World, Bessie can identify with the patriarchal definition of women as wives and mothers.

Bessie forges a new identity and adjusts painfully to an alien way of life, entirely for the sake of her daughters. As part of the 'immigrant exile' motif, Bessie projects her hopes onto her children who represent both a link with the old country and a future in the new country.

> Dispossessed though they were, needing to cling to and preserve memories of the old world, they yet hungrily claimed personal shares of experience, of opportunity, of Canada. Above all, amid mutilations of communal and religious life, they worked to provide a home and an education for their children who would be the 'real Canadians.'[5]

It is only in the hospital, in solitude, that Bessie begins to think of herself separately from her family. Bessie's inner reflections give her the required distance to reclaim her autonomy detached from others. But when her daughters visit her, Bessie is brought back to the social responsibilities of her position as mother. In this vein, Annie describes her own children's achievements, how her son Steve is captain of the baseball team and how her son Allan is first in his class. Bessie is disappointed that Judy's children go to Catholic school and will grow up thinking that "Chanuka is a Japanese toy." (15) Although Bessie regrets that her grandchildren will lose their Jewish heritage, she appreciates the financial security her son-in-law brings and the private nurse he has hired for her. Bessie and her daughters want to retain social appearances and protect one another from the pain of failed expectations. Bessie wants her daughters to believe she is getting better and they try to convince their mother they are succeeding in life. When Sheila tells her mother that her book will be published, Bessie in turn feigns satisfaction.

OLD BESSIE: They're going to print it! And sell it in all the stores! You see, Alex, she's going to be all right. For that I give you a kiss, Sheila. (Bessie kisses her) That's all I want. My children should be settled and have 'naches' from life. (15)

It is only when Bessie is alone again and retreats into her younger consciousness that she deliberates on how she undermined her daughters' ambitions. She recalls how Judy comes home one day and announces that she wants to go to New York to become an actress. Young Bessie refuses to let her go.

YOUNG BESSIE: ...I'm not going to let you ruin your life...Judy, pity me! You're my treasure. For this I work like a slave? For you to walk the streets in a strange city?

JUDY: Mama, I want to be somebody!

YOUNG BESSIE: When you have bread on the table, you can afford to be somebody. You'll get married first, to a nice boy, with a good job, if he wants you to be an actress, you'll be an actress. In the meantime, you'll stay home. (16)

The prototypal Jewish mother, both self-sacrificing and controlling, Bessie lives vicariously through her daughters, treating them as possessions. Her panic mounts as the persona of Young Bessie invades her conscious mind. Gone at the stroke of the auctioneer's hammer, she sees the candlesticks disappear, a symbol of a vanished world and her lost family, provoking her to cry: "That'll never happen to my children! Never!" (16) Rich writes about the "double vision"[6] in regard to the Jewish mother: she is viewed with contempt and resentment on the one hand, and admiration and reverence on the other.

> But there is also a smouldering energy and resilience in the domesticated Jewish woman which—from a woman's point of view—commands respect, however it has been abused or derogated by this particular subculture. She is a survivor-woman, a fighter with tooth and claw and her own nervous

system, who, like her black sisters, has borne the weight of a people on her back.[7]

In her struggle to survive, however, Old Bessie has denied her own self-development for the sake of her children. By viewing marriage as the only promise for a successful future, she endorses the old-world traditions of patriarchy, seeing her daughters as an extension of her own self-denial.

Margaret Atwood perceives women in Canadian literature as falling into two main categories: "The Diana or Maiden figure, the young girl," or "the Hecate figure" personified as "the goddess of the underworld, who presides over death and has oracular powers."[8] The mothers in Sheila Watson's *The Double Hook,* Hollingsworth's *Mother Country,* and Joudry's *Mother is Watching* are such examples of Canada's life-denying female literary figures.

> If you trusted Canadian fiction you would have to believe that most of the women in the country with any real presence at all are over fifty, and a tough, sterile, suppressed and granite-jawed lot they are. They live their lives with intensity, but through gritted teeth, and they are often seen as malevolent, sinister or life-denying, either by themselves or by other characters in their books.[9]

Although Bessie possesses the controlling characteristics of the 'Hecate' figure, her approaching death is not destructive, but rather, life-affirming. Her stifled individuality becomes illuminated by her vibrant self beneath the socially defined role as mother, wife, and old woman. She remembers herself as a young woman at a dance with an old boyfriend. "Sh. Laibel, the old woman is very sick. Look what's become of her, poor thing." (18) Laibel replies, "You'll never be old for me, Bessie. I'll always remember you like this." The hiatus between the young persona and the old woman she has become, leads Bessie to repudiate her own deterioration towards death. Like the aging mother in Monro's "The Peace of Utrecht," Bessie is trapped in a role over which she has no control. Bessie seeks the self-realization which will transcend the social restrictions of her position as a dying old woman. Like the heroine in Maillet's *La Sagouine*, Bessie's identification with her younger self expresses her search for her female potential and autonomy beyond physical boundaries. Young Bessie, as the 'Venus' figure, is a sensual being, an erotic figure who breaks out of her social role as wife and mother by having an affair. Young Bessie is transposed by Laibel's fantasy of taking her away to California to live in luxury, in "the real land of milk and honey." (18)

Bessie returns to the present, confusing it with the past. She remembers with horror Alex discovering the affair and running out of the house in anger. Old Bessie calls for Alex, believing he has left her, but he is sitting beside her, comforting her through her illness. Alex is characterized as a gentle, but unambitious man. He is not the powerful male persona of the patriarchal tradition; rather, it is Old Bessie who shows intense concern for the future of the family. She is the strong one, the one who makes the decisions, although she is motivated by the desire to see her daughters successfully married. As Janeway observes, "the less control which a woman exercises over other areas of her life, the greater will be the satisfaction she derives from managing the lives of her children."[10] Because Bessie's world is that of wife and mother, her sense of power is contained within the domestic realm where she directs the lives of her offspring.

Through her fragmented state of consciousness, Old Bessie begins to attain insight into the human condition. She tells the nurse about the importance of living a good life, as one must relive everything through memory.

OLD BESSIE: So I want to tell you something. Everything you live
               now, you'll live again when you're old. It'll only
               be in your head, but just as real as the first time.

So do nice things, Angela, so your last days will be
nice. (20)

In a private meeting with her daughter, Annie, Old Bessie is concerned that Annie is overworked, but she worries most that her husband,
Harry, will leave her because she has no time to take care of her appearance.

OLD BESSIE: Ah, Annie, we live everyday worrying about the
               future. But what happens to today, to now? The
               years go in the garbage and there's nothing left
               but a bundle of garbage...If you don't watch out,
               Harry's going to find a young girl with red cheeks
               and lots of 'koyach'. (21)

Old Bessie gives Annie money to spend on improving her appearance:
"You stop working today, you hear? Go to the beauty parlour; buy a few
dresses. It's a shame the way you go round in that coat." (21) She paints a
picture of women as defined by stereotypes: that working outside the
home will lead to the breakdown of the family. But Annie's state of
exhaustion is a result of fulfilling two roles: that of economic provider and
housewife.

Although Old Bessie wants to secure her daughters' happiness, she
cannot perceive their existence outside the traditional role of women. She
shows her self-sacrificing nature, giving up her own needs for the benefit
of her daughters' marital security.

OLD BESSIE: All my life I worked, not for myself. When you grew up,
               to buy the grandchildren presents, to dress nice
               you shouldn't be ashamed of me. Now, it's all
               finished... (21)

In Bessie's old age, illness and solitude, she questions her self-identity for the first time, free from the intrusion of social responsibility. On the subject of women's servitude to others, Miller observes,

> Women are taught that their main goal in life is to serve others—first men, and later, children. This prescription leads to enormous problems, for it is supposed to be carried out as if women did not have needs of their own, as if one could serve others without simultaneously attending to one's own interests and desires.[11]

As Old Bessie slips into her inner psyche, she begins to comprehend that self-sacrificing is a form of control. By serving others and denying her own existence, she is unable to fully understand the needs of others.

OLD BESSIE: The children need you like a hole in the head.
YOUNG BESSIE: They'll always need me.
OLD BESSIE: They never did what they wanted.
YOUNG BESSIE: This country gave us a home, a place to live in peace, as Jews. What more could they want?
OLD BESSIE: You know what I mean.
YOUNG BESSIE: Annie has a good husband, she's all right.
OLD BESSIE: All right is not good enough. (22)

Old Bessie begins to realize that acquiring identity is more complex than simply accepting the conventional role of wife and mother. She becomes aware of the potential for individuality beyond the limitations of social expectations; a perception she refused to acknowledge when her children were growing up.

Young Bessie is unaware of the opportunities for self-development offered by the New World as a setting where her daughters could realize their individual potential. Instead, Young Bessie limits her daughters' future to the typical role of homemaker. To Young Bessie, Canada is a secure place to raise her children, not a land of opportunity for educating her daughters. She refuses adamantly to allow Annie to attend university.

YOUNG BESSIE: You'll go to business college, then work in an office…

ANNIE: I'd rather die.

YOUNG BESSIE: I wish I had the education to work in an office. You don't break your back, nice men come in, maybe the boss's son…

ANNIE: I want to study!

YOUNG BESSIE: You want, I also want lots of things. Maybe if you were a boy, it would be different. Now we'll save up money, get a nice place for you and Judy to bring your boyfriends…

ANNIE: (Runs out crying) Mama, you make me sick! (24)

Annie's development is cloistered by Bessie's definition of her as a woman. Annie is forced to perceive her self-identity through the limitations of the patriarchal system, which excludes women going to university and becoming scientists. Janeway writes about the shift away from patriarchal values and the turmoil created when the old customs are challenged. The "structure of myth declares itself to be eternal and always present, the old call the young immoral, and the young reject the old as hypocrites."[12]

Bessie's need to cling to her traditional moral values is concomitant with her retainment of Jewish heritage. Her lack of vision concerning her daughters' positions as women is tied to her perception of her own self growing up in Russia where marriage was seen as a form of survival. To Bessie, Annie's scholarship is meaningless because it does not lead to marriage.

Back in the present, reflecting on Annie's unfulfilled ambitions triggers the memory of Bessie's own failed potential.

OLD BESSIE: In my town girls were lucky if they learned to read and write...If I had the chance, wonder what I could have been...a teacher, a bookkeeper... (25)

Rich analyzes how a mother's self-denial affects her relationship with her daughter who struggles to free herself from the self-sacrificing nature of her mother "through whom the restrictions and degradations of a female existence were perforce transmitted."[13]

Bessie sinks back into the past and remembers the table set for Passover, a symbol of her Jewish heritage. Sheila disrupts this religious ceremony by demanding a piece of 'matsah' while her father is praying over wine. When Annie gets the prized matsah instead of herself, Sheila blurts out "Shit!" (27) Alex, horrified by his daughter's lack of respect for Jewish tradition, commands her to leave.

YOUNG ALEX: (To Sheila) Get away from the table.
SHEILA: (Protesting) Papa!
YOUNG ALEX: Out I said! (27)

It is at this moment that Sheila runs into the alley and gets raped by a gang of boys. The act of rape represents the corruption of the outside world which threatens the moral and religious fibre of Bessie's family, and also suggests Sheila's condemnation by her father. The religious connotation here is that of Alex as the Divine Patriarch banishing his sinful daughter Eve from the garden of Eden where she is forced to contend with a hostile, alien land.

When Sheila comes to visit Bessie in the hospital, she reveals her feelings of failure. Her longing for something meaningful makes her dream of going to Europe. For the first time, Bessie tells Sheila about the importance of self-fulfillment and the discovery of her individuality. "If going away will make you happy, I'm happy." (29)

Through her introspection on the threshold of death Bessie begins to transmit her reflections to her daughters. Aviva Ravel explores the process of dying as a transforming experience, "only at the moment of death do you separate reality from fantasy and come closest to the true essence of your person."[14] Through her impending death, Bessie is finally able to disengage her individual identity from social expectations.

When Bessie is alone again, she realizes that Sheila will not find what she is looking for by changing environments, for she must attain inner meaning first.

OLD BESSIE: (Holds up her hand) You see this hand? No matter which finger you cut off, they all hurt the same...the trouble is, child, you won't find what you want, not in Europe, not in Africa, and that's why I cry, not for myself, Gottenu, not for myself... (29)

This realization leads Bessie back into her younger consciousness, as she recalls the day Sheila came home after being raped in the alley. The older, wiser Bessie tries to make the younger Bessie acknowledge her negligence. Young Bessie, on the other hand, declares she had too many responsibilities to cope with.

OLD BESSIE: She had no business being out on the street at night.
YOUNG BESSIE: She had a fight with Alex. She tore his book. He yelled and she ran out. I was too busy to go after her. How was I to know that...
OLD BESSIE: You also loved the others more.

YOUNG BESSIE: No! I had to keep peace in the house. The two of
them always shouting at each other. I had to keep
peace! (30)

Ravel suggests women's inability to be solely responsible for the care of others when they alone must keep the family together. Miller articulates this claim when she writes:

In a system which so totally constricted women, mothers could not possibly give their daughters what the daughters needed, as they did not receive what they needed as mothers.[15]

The more Old Bessie connects with her younger self, the greater understanding she obtains of her own life and of the human condition. Old Bessie meditates upon the final peace that death will bring and the acceptance of destiny: life will go on after she is gone. "Day and night, summer—winter. People are born, they get married..." (30)

Bessie tries to reconcile herself with Judy's marriage and the recognition that her daughter's roots are in the New World. She remembers Judy's wedding when she tried to make Alex accept that "Times are different." (30) Although Judy has married a gentile and lost much of her heritage, she has married a man who is affluent enough to support the entire family, and has acquired the material security Bessie has always craved for her daughters. Although Bessie displays a realistic acceptance of life, it is shown to be tinged with irony.

OLD BESSIE: By me, whenever something good happens, it has to
have a little bad too. Nu, maybe it'll be all
right. And if not, she can always come back to
Mama. (31)

Bessie's contemplation sets the stage for the discussion on the telephone with Judy. Judy tells Bessie that her daughter, Cathy, ran away, to get away from the "phoniness" of life. Cathy's search for meaning inspires Judy to question her own identity. Judy discloses that she too would like to get away from the artificiality of her life. Bessie, now aware of the importance of self-fulfillment and spontaneity, tells Judy to go off by herself if that is what she wishes. "So get yourself a knapsack and start hitch-hiking." (31)

Through her old age and accompanying illness, Bessie perceives human existence in a new light. June Singer sees old age as a period of enlightenment, free from social obligation.

> In old age, when people have already proved their identity and established their position in the world, there is no longer so much necessity to live by collective standards. It is a time when those who have fulfilled the objective purposes for which they have striven are ready to turn inward and let themselves be more what they truly are and less what the world expects.[16]

Through her reflections, Bessie discovers the ambiguity of marriage—that people spend their lives together because they are afraid to die alone. The paradox is that death must be faced alone, by everyone. "I can't...stop...it's so funny...live a whole life together so you don't die alone!" (32) Bessie's revelation of life's absurdity makes her laugh until she is filled with pain and the nurse is summoned by Alex to give her an injection. Bessie is put in a deep sleep and begins to dream about her three daughters again. Her worst fears are brought to life as the auctioneer, a symbol of her lost heritage, introduces Judy at a nightclub where she sings "Paper Doll."

JUDY: (Sings) "I want a paper doll that I can call my own. A doll that other fellahs cannot steal. And then the flirty flirty guys

with the flirty flirty eyes will have to flirt with dollies
that are real..." (32)

The lyrics of the song express Bessie's fear that Judy would become a victim
of male exploitation in the corrupt world of urban night life. Bessie's
struggle for survival in Russia in the face of annihilation is interwoven
with her struggle to keep her daughters safe from the hostile forces of
Canadian metropolitan society. The Jewish tradition that had been
threatened by anti-semitism in Russia is replaced by a different kind of
danger: that of material values and the alienation they produce. Annie is
seen typing a business letter, and Sheila, in a mental institution, recites a
poem about despair.

> The walls are covered with thick slime. I touched them
> accidentally and my fingers are caught in the mess. I pull
> with all my might but the stuff drips from my hand, like from
> a leaky faucet. There is no place to run, for my legs sink in the
> sewage... (32)

Bessie's consciousness becomes fragmented as she desperately hangs on to
her traditional beliefs in the face of the modern world's chaos.

ANNIE:	No choices...
JUDY:	Be somebody...
OLD ALEX:	Leave me, Bessie, leave me... (Young Bessie dances in with Young Alex.)
YOUNG BESSIE:	If only life were one long dance. (33)

The different streams of consciousness overlap as Bessie tries to make sense
out of her own identity. "I did everything for you! Where would you have
been without me?...but I forgot to live myself." (33) Young Bessie uncovers
another paradox—that life must end when one begins to understand the

world, and sees that Old Bessie needs more time to make up for her past mistakes. "Let her live a little longer. She has things to fix up. So much to do!" (33)

Alex enters Bessie's dream state and voices his traumatic experiences as a young boy, witnessing soldiers murdering his family.

YOUNG ALEX: I wanted you to have an easy life, Bessie. But I was afraid of rich men, politicians, goyim. When I was a little boy, the soldiers came into our village. They burned the houses. Then they came to our house. They stabbed my mother six times, she fell on the floor and died. My older brother ran out in the street to fight them with his bare hands. They shot him. I hid in the cupboard. At night I ran away. A man took me across the border in a wagon of straw… Since then I've been afraid. (33)

The cruelty and sense of loss is magnified through the laughter of their three daughters and the auctioneer. Their daughters, identifying with Canadian experience, are perceived as indifferent to their parents' past suffering and loss of culture. Although Alex and Bessie have managed to escape the destruction of their past existence, what they find in their new setting is a society that threatens their heritage through assimilation. As part of the dislocation felt by the immigrant, the Jew, as the 'perennial exile' epitomizes the struggle for identity.

Burdened by old-world attitudes and influences, yet struggling to be accepted by and to accept the not always understood or even desired new culture, the Jew walked a tightrope, balancing the remembered claims of his forefathers and the ambiguous demands of the alien environment. He was the proverbial stranger in a strange and harsh land.[17]

Although Canada may offer peace and security to immigrants, it can also separate them from their cultural, historical, and moral traditions. Bessie, preparing to go into surgery, articulates this disjunction.

OLD BESSIE: Listen to me nurse. I was a young girl in a strange country. I didn't know the language. My little town had only three streets. I knew everybody. I never understood America. Too many people, too much work. I did my best. I made Shabbos for the family. 'Yom-Tov' was 'Yom- Tov' I was a good Jewish daughter. I did my best!(33)

As Bessie reminisces about her personal sense of loss, she voices her exclusion and disorientation as a Jew, immigrant, and woman struggling to achieve integration. She realizes that "it doesn't matter in the end. You're alone anyway. The pain, the fear, everything is lived alone." (35)

There is a sense of sadness at the end of the play, but it is combined with an acceptance and understanding of loss. Through her approaching death, Bessie obtains the ultimate connection with her own self, free from the constraints of the external world. The tragic dimensions of the play suggest that although Bessie's illness culminates in death, it has brought about a deeper awareness of her own individuality. Juxtaposing Bessie's insight at the moment of death, however, is her sudden vision of the Russian auctioneer selling the family candlesticks for one million rubles. Paradoxically, spiritual victory has been gained, but not without the realization that Bessie's traditional inheritance has been lost to the materialism of the modern world.

NOTES

1. Newton, Elaine. "Forward" to *Mirror of a People: Canadian Jewish Experience in Poetry and Prose*, eds. Sheldon Oberman and Elaine Newton, Winnipeg: Jewish Educational Publishers of Canada Inc. 1985, p. xiv.
2. Ibid. p. xiv.
3. Rich. pp. 235-236.
4. Moss. p. 83.
5. Newton and Oberman. p. 2.
6. Rich. p. 203.
7. Ibid.
8. Atwood. *Survival*, p. 199.
9. Ibid.
10. Janeway. p. 54.
11. Miller. p. 62.
12. Janeway. p. 140.
13. Rich. p.235.
14. Morley, Patricia. "Talking with Aviva Ravel, on Priorities, Fairness, and Being Human," *Canadian Drama*, (Fall 1979) p. 186.
15. Miller. p. 139.
16. Singer, June. *Androgyny: Toward a New Theory of Sexuality*, Garden City, N.Y: Anchor Press, 1976. p. 321.
17. Newton. p. xv.

V

A Place on Earth

In *A Place on Earth,* as in *The Twisted Loaf,* the search for female identity is explored within the boundaries of an urban landscape. Densely populated Toronto becomes a metaphorical wilderness where the sense of dislocation and isolation is manifested by an urban wasteland.

Canadian women playwrights frequently use an urban setting as symbolic of both female inner landscape and exclusion from the male world. Beverley Simons' play, *Crabdance,* Lezley Havard's *Despair,* Margaret Penman's *Wheelchair* and Elinore Siminovitch's *Tomorrow and Tomorrow* all examine women's disembodiment from urban, male society through their isolation, loneliness and lack of power.

In *A Place on Earth,* produced in 1982, Betty Jane Wylie, through her protagonist, Peggy, suggests that effacement of female identity becomes more all-encompassing in the urban wilderness of pre-cast concrete than it does in the untamed, primeval world of nature. The unchartered forest may intimidate, even annihilate, but it can also restore primordial roots, tap hidden resources within, as shown in *Islands,* where, unlike the city, nature enhances individual growth. Peggy, a seventy-two year old widow, fights for survival and dignity in the inimical world of the inner city. Her isolation, symbolized by her shabby one-room apartment, is her only refuge against the savage cruelty of the ghettoized chaos outside her door.

The "unconscious horror of nature,"[1] prevalent in dramatic works like Ringwood's *Still Stands the House* and Hollingsworth's *Ever Loving,* is transformed in *A Place on Earth* to a terror evoked by the concrete urban jungle. Where the wilderness in the former plays accentuates female powerlessness in facing both nature and the repressions of patriarchal society, in the latter play, female alienation in the inner city has been artificially created by man. What is threatening to Peggy is not the savagery of winter or wild animals found in the wilderness, but the fear of male violence lurking in the dark streets. To emphasize this outside threat, the play describes the male activities in the hall which disturb Peggy's tranquillity.

> We hear men's voices grunting, greeting each other. We hear
> a good, productive cough, retrieval, and a toilet flushing.
> The body in the bed becomes restless, resisting all this noise,
> turning away from it, pulling the covers more tightly around
> her head. (1)

As a woman alone, her world of fear is personified as the male world in which Peggy is victimized through rape. She is further demoralized by the indifference of the police and by the drunken men lurking outside her apartment door. The hostile urban environment, unlike the forest which frightens Ruth and Diana in *Ever Loving,* is shown to be man-made. Alienation and fear in *A Place on Earth* are derived from male aggression manifested in the urban setting through the actions of men who govern it.

As an expression of male power, D. G. Jones sees the technological, urban reality as an attempt to conquer and subject the forces of nature.

> In extremes he has declared total war on the wilderness,
> woman, or the world of spontaneous impulse and irrational
> desire. At the least he has sought to subjugate these unruly

elements within himself by force of will. More largely, he has sought to bind them in the body politic by force of law. And more ambitious still, with the increased confidence in his power, he has sought to control them in the world around him and even to eradicate them from the earth.[2]

Peggy, as part of the natural elements man wishes to subjugate, fights for survival in the engulfing body politic. As a way of defining her existence, Peggy maintains her inner, emotional world through her puppet, Buddy. This dramatic device connects Peggy with her inner consciousness and allows for the articulation of her individuality in opposition to the indifferent, mechanical outside world. The puppet is also a personification of the artistic, imaginative world in which Peggy finds refuge. Through nursery rhymes, the puppet connects Peggy with her meaningful past when she was an elementary school teacher and made puppets for her students. In her state of solitude, the puppet is instrumental in making everyday life an aesthetic experience and gives trivial daily activities a level of fantasy, as together they sing nursery rhymes.

PEGGY: (sings) Make the bed,
           Shake the bed,
           Turn the bed right over.
           Make the bed, shake the bed,
           Turn the bed right over. (3)

This nursery rhyme also suggests Peggy's search for identity outside the traditional role of wife and mother. Peggy confronts the limited position of women in the home by appropriating her domestic setting and transforming it into her private space. By wanting to "shake the bed," and "turn the bed right over," Wylie portrays a symbolic revolution whereby Peggy overthrows the patriarchal throne. The act of 'making' the bed becomes a reshaping of traditional forms, culminating in the transfiguration of the androcentric approach, again by turning the bed "right over."

As Peggy makes her morning tea, the puppet sings "Polly put the kettle on" and "Jack be nimble." Nursery rhymes serve to give creative significance to the mundane, as, in her solitude, Peggy performs her domestic chores as a ritual, no longer as a duty. The puppet also helps Peggy keep her individuality and sense of dignity which she struggles to restore after the degradation of rape.

VOICE: I always said you were a lady.

PEGGY: (suddenly angry) And where did that get me? Exposed, and ripped, and invaded. Oh! Oh!
    (She shudders and shakes and stops and stares into space)

VOICE: This won't do, Peggy.

PEGGY: I know, I know. (6)

While Peggy prepares her breakfast, a woman phones her about a survey. As an expression of the hostility of the outside world, the woman bang downs the phone when she discovers Peggy is retired and over sixty, giving her the feeling she is unimportant in society. "I don't count!" (7) However, contrary to this perception, Peggy defines her own position:

PEGGY: I have *not* retired. Soon, maybe, but not yet. I still work. I work very hard. I work very hard at staying alive. I work very hard at finding the truth of each day...I may retire. I'll have to think about that. (8)

The phone call leads Peggy to think about her relation to others, as the telephone has become her only source of human contact with her friends and family. This heightens her sense of insecurity in the technological urban reality where communication has become automatous, severed from emotional involvement. "Phone calls like that make you wonder why you have a phone. Why *do* I have a phone? Because Marion pays for it, that's why." (8) Buddy reminds Peggy how the telephone allows her to keep in touch with her daughter, Marion and friends like Lily and Madge. But Peggy finds she is still alienated from her friends: Lily's asthma which prevents her from talking, and the possessiveness of Madge's husband. "I can't ever talk to her too long because Harry gets jealous." (8)

In reflecting about her married friend, Madge, Peggy recalls her own domestic duties as a traditional wife, and acts out a marriage scenario to Buddy.

> Would you like some more tea, dear? How about a nice Arrowroot bickie, love? Want me to cut your meat? (pause) Oh, no. No...he could cut his own meat. But more clothes to wash. Oh, my. It's all I can do to look after myself. I don't know how Madge does it. (9)

Peggy reveals how her position as wife included being mother and hand-maiden to her husband, and finds her friendship with Madge a meaningful reminder of her marriage. "She gives me glimpses of the world I left behind." (9)

Through her friend Alma, Peggy can identify with her strong, inde-pendent self. As a college student, Alma evokes happy memories of Peggy's own student days when she fell in love with Herb, the principal, whom she married. She contemplates her perception of self and how much she has changed over the years. Like Bessie in *The Twisted Loaf,* Peggy's external image in the mirror contrasts with her inner vision of herself. "Who is that old hag? (pause) Not me. That's not whom I remember. I don't know you. I don't know you at all." (10) Like Bessie, Peggy finds affinity with her young, vibrant self, and fears her older self as destructive and repellent, for she has internalized stereotyped images of old women. De Beauvoir describes society's negative images of old women: "it takes only the passage of time to alter her charms—infirm, homely, old, woman is horrifying."[3]

101

While Peggy prepares herself to go to the police station to press charges, she judges her appearance in the context of the fairy tales she learned as a young girl. As she brushes her hair, she imagines herself as a young, beautiful Rapunzel figure. "And who did you used to be? (pause) Rapunzel, Rapunzel, let down your golden hair!" (11) But Peggy reinterprets the romantic illusion to suit her own life, where the "handsome prince" dies and leaves Rapunzel a poor widow. "And after that? (pause) He died, he died. (pause) And she lived...forever after. There!" (11)

In Peggy's search for self-definition, the mirror reflects Peggy's self-doubts about her appearance, and simultaneously it becomes a symbol for male images of female beauty, ones Peggy no longer lives up to. "Mirror, mirror, on the wall, Who's the oldest of them all?" (12) Susan Griffin writes about the mirror as a metonym for the male perception of female beauty. In the "room of the dressing where the walls are covered with mirrors. Where mirrors are like eyes of men, and the women reflect the judgments of mirrors."[4] Peggy is confronted with socially created images of women in the mirror, unable to see her real self.

As Peggy wonders how she is perceived extrinsically through her reflection in the mirror, she decides to phone the police station to alert them of her visit. She is then haunted by her traumatic rape experience, riveted to her memory.

> ...I really thought he was going to kill me. This is it, I thought. It's not so bad. This is it. Rough. Strong. Pressure. Dragging me down, arm over my face. And then his knees in my ribs. Ripping, tearing. Clothes. Flesh. Dry. Tearing. (pause) Don't think about it, don't think about it...(pause) Yes, I remember him. (13)

Although Peggy tries to go on with her life, the rape experience has destroyed her self-esteem. Griffin, in her analysis of rape, equates it with the annihilation of selfhood into non-being.

In the moment of rape a woman becomes anonymous. Like all victims of terrorism, there is something awesomely accidental about her fate. She is like the duck flying in formation which the hunter chose to shoot down—she appeared in his gunsight. Absorbed by his violence, her soul and the history of her soul are lost, are irrelevant.[5]

Rosemary Radford Ruether perceives the act of rape as an expression of man's desire to dominate the earth, subduing all "inferior" existence into products of consumption. "Through the raped bodies the earth is raped. Those who enjoy the goods distance themselves from the destruction."[6]

Peggy repudiates her feelings of insignificance by concentrating on her daily activities which are performed like rituals, celebrating her individual survival. As she does her exercises, she uses her cane to perform a tap dance and imagines how she could have defended herself against her attacker. "Hit him with your cane, Peg! Just hit him with your cane next time. Belt him!" (15)

Another activity that gives Peggy pleasure is opening her mail. She finds a letter from her cousin, Laura, who tells her that her aunt is very ill. Peggy remembers her childhood when her young and beautiful aunt used to put nail polish on Peggy's toe nails. Now her aunt is old and close to death. "And now she's…dear God—she's ninety!" (18) This realization fills Peggy with horror, as she ponders her own state of decline through old age and loneliness. "Oh, Buddy! Stay with me! Stay with me!" (18) Peggy then reads a letter from her granddaughter, Debby, which only intensifies her state of loneliness.

Unlike the solitude of Muriel in *Islands,* Peggy does not choose to be alone. Where Muriel believes it is the political system that forces people to live together, Peggy finds it is the structure of society that isolates people from loved ones. "There must be something wrong with a system that separates grandmothers from their grandchildren." (18) Although Peggy cannot visit Debby, who has sent her fangs for Halloween, she interacts with Debby on the level of imagination, through nursery rhymes and ritual. Peggy puts on the fangs and plays the part of a witch.

> Wicked Old Witch,
> Are you hungry today?
> If you are—
> Then we will run away. (18)

Another source of inspiration is Peggy's drawer filled with souvenirs from the past, like her old birthday cards. Peggy's memory is stirred by vivid recollections of love and sensuality. But these sensations are smothered by the brutality of rape.

> ...I remember how wonderful it was to be touched, to be held. Everyone needs to be touched...But not like that, not like that! (She starts to rock back and forth) That ...was an act of violence, against my body. Against my spirit. Violation. I was inviolate and I was taken in violence. Ripped and torn. Torn apart! (20)

Peggy rips up one of her birthday cards, representing the annihilation of her being through her violent attack.

She retrieves her late husband's cap from World War I, her teacher's certificate, and her marriage license. These are all meaningful symbols in her life, uniting her with the past as well as being rich sources of inspiration in defining her present existence. Through her husband's photograph, Peggy awakens the memory of her intimate and poetic relationship with her husband.

> Herbert Woodgreen, you could charm the birds out of the trees. It never mattered that we didn't have much money. We

used to pop corn and do jigsaw puzzles and read poetry and
make love, and laugh. Oh, and laugh! (21)

By becoming a widow, Peggy has no control over her state of solitude
which is inflicted upon her, as Singer suggests when writing about
widowhood and female-identity. "The woman who has defined herself
and her personality in terms of her relationship to a man suffers most when
she is faced with widowhood. Unlike the divorcee, she has not deliberately
chosen the path of self-determination..."[7]

As a widow, Peggy's status as an autonomous woman is ruptured by
her deeply embedded loneliness due to the death of her husband and other
loved ones. The birth certificates of her two children, John and Marion,
remind her of her role as a mother, and a newspaper clipping brings back
her son's death in a car accident. Another clipping describes her husband's
death, leaving her to struggle alone. Herb's obituary reads, "survived by
his wife." (22) This makes Peggy consider her individual struggle for
identity in the midst of isolation and loss. "I always knew I was a survivor."
However, she feels it is not enough "merely to have survived!" For, unlike
Muriel in *Islands*, Peggy craves to have her family back again. Peggy sees
her state of solitude as her banishment from all that is meaningful, and it is
only through fading memories that she is able to anchor her past to the
present. "I keep burying parts of myself—people I loved, memories. It's
getting so I know more people in the cemetery than on the street." (23) In
her reclusion, Peggy imagines what it would be like if some of her dead
loved ones could come back to be with her, just for one day.

In contrast with her rich and meaningful past relationships, Peggy
now has only fragmentary and sporadic connections with others. A volun-
teer comes by to give Peggy a "meals on wheels" lunch, leaving it outside
her door; she plays a Halloween game from her window with the children
in the street by putting on her fangs and playing the part of a witch.
Peggy's daily activities are an attempt to re-create her identity in the face of
desperate loneliness. As Singer observes of the widow:

A widow finds herself in a position in which she is nearly forced to develop her own creative powers in order to fill the missing part of her own existence with something to make her feel whole again. If she succeeds in this, she reaches a new level of conscious development.[8]

In an attempt to fill the void in her life, Peggy always observes the "niceties." She sets the dinner table with care, and always puts on clean clothes. Maintaining a level of dignity is related to Peggy's self-affirmation. But beneath the surface, Peggy's feelings of mortification emerge as she catches a glimpse of herself in the mirror.

I hate you! You sit there so cold, watching, watching, aging, aging, but never a crack in the facade. Cold and icy, and every day one day older. Stop it! (25)

Like Bessie in *The Twisted Loaf*, Peggy keeps seeing her outward self as a frightening stranger. Peggy, too, seeks her young and vital self behind the deteriorating mask of old age. As part of the "Nature-Woman" motif described by Atwood, Peggy perceives herself as both destructive and life-affirming, fluctuating between the two polarities. Like Hagar Shipley in *The Stone Angel*, Peggy's young and creative self is trapped inside a malignant image of decay from which she tries to liberate herself. *A Place on Earth* reflects Peggy's struggle to free herself from the negative perceptions of old age by identifying with her inner world of imagination. The play delves into Peggy's fragmented consciousness, one that swings from a sense of integration to a level of disintegration and self-alienation. As Peggy eats her lunch she throws custard at the shrivelled mirror image of her old self, wishing the intruder would go away. "I'm not looking at you. You're not my friend..." (26) Then Peggy is brought back to reality as Buddy scolds her like a young child, pointing out the mess she has to clean up. Peggy's sense of humour is restored, and she remarks, "That's the worst of being a woman. You always have to clean up after yourself." (26) Peggy believes in the importance of individual responsibility which she used to teach her children. "That's what I used to tell my kids. Be responsible." (27)

As Peggy cleans up, she recalls her role as a traditional wife and Herb's unwillingness to help in the house, which Peggy now sees as irresponsibility. "Now, Herb, there, he never picked up after himself at all. That man—may he rest in peace—was a SLOB!" (27) As Peggy finishes her cleaning, she is shown to be in good humour. However, when she catches her reflection in the mirror, she digresses to a negative perception of herself.

> So many lines to learn. Where did they all come from? If only the me that was, was still in there. Where are you Peggy? Where did you go—I saw you just a little while ago, looking bright and fresh and full of wonder...Well, you're still full of wonder. (27)

Peggy tries to find her creative, eternal self which she knows is buried deep within her, a timeless self, governed by imagination and wonder. Griffin writes about the potential of seeing beyond stereotyped images to the primeval sources which unite all women.

> And now, beneath these images we can see the gleam of older images. And these peel back to reveal the older still. The past, the dead, once breathing, the forgotten, the secret, the buried, the once blood and bone, the vanished, shimmering now like an answer from these walls...[9]

However, Peggy's consciousness shifts back to conventional images of women as she paints her face to go outside. Buddy echoes social customs and their definition of femininity. "A girl's face is her fortune." (28) Peggy identifies with her younger self as an erotic being, "the loving, potentially beautiful woman trapped inside a negative shell."[10] As she dresses up, she ignites the embers of her romantic vision as a young woman in love. "My love, you are like a cameo. Oh, Herbert, how loving you are! Oh, my love, oh, my love." In this state of mind, Peggy abruptly leaves the seclusion of her apartment, ready to confront the outside world.

In Act II, Peggy's experience at the police department is revealed through a telephone conversation with her daughter, Marion. The cruel malice of the police towards Peggy's rape experience augments her position as victim in the world of male violence, a position Peggy challenges.

> ...Then they asked what I was doing out that time of night. Eight o'clock on a Saturday night, what was I doing out? I was going to the drugstore, to buy some popcorn. I like popcorn. Why not ask that man what was *he* doing out? They should have a curfew for men. Then women would be safe on the streets... (32)

Peggy confronts the authority of the police who, by their apathy, condone the abuse of women. This reiterates Griffin's claim that rape is a form of "mass terrorism"[11] which subjects women to male control.

> [T]he victims of rape are chosen indiscriminately, but the propagandists for male supremacy broadcast that it is women who cause rape by being unchaste or in the wrong place at the wrong time—in essence, by behaving as though they were free.[12]

Peggy describes how the police conceive her sexual assault as an acceptable part of male behaviour:

...I heard one of the men say to another one—I guess he
thought I couldn't hear—he said he'd been wondering how
long it was since an old prune like me had had some fresh
meat... (32)

The policemen's perception of women demonstrates how they see
women as "the Other,"[13] thus divided from male experience. As de
Beauvoir observes, because women have been outside the realm of male
activity, they have been perceived in conjunction with nature. And just as
man asserts his will on nature, he projects his consciousness on women.

Now ally, now enemy, she appears as the dark chaos from
whence life wells up, as this life itself, and as the over-yonder
toward which life tends. Woman sums up nature as Mother,
Wife, and Idea; these forms now mingle and now conflict,
and each of them wears a double visage.[14]

As part of this double visage of women, the rape victim is woman as
enemy, who must be subjugated. By going to the police station to press
charges against her attacker, Peggy wishes to eradicate the perception of
women as "the Other," integrating female experience into the political
power structures. However, she finds as a woman and rape victim, she is
denied recognition as an equal.

I was going to fight for justice and stand up for all women,
my last act of bravery, and they bruised my spirit as badly as
that creature bruised my body... (32)

To emphasize the hostility of her surroundings, a man tries to get
through Peggy's door which she has left open. He calls her "sweet-
heart" and asks her if she wants a drink. Instead, Peggy decides to pour
her own drink and celebrate her pursuit of justice. As she makes pop-

corn, Peggy ruminates on her marginalized position as widow and scapegoat.

> Men...develop...*nasty habits!* (pause) So they leave. Leave us
> holding the bag. Ex...it. Here's to all the little old ladies left
> holding the bag...And there shall rise...a mighty popping
> ...of corn! (34)

She envisions a mock revolution whereby old women rebel against their exclusion from society and assert their individual power.

> Witches, unite! You have nothing to lose but your brooms!
> (sips again) Bring back brooms and cats for little old ladies!
> (sips again) Grandmothers of the world—hit 'em with your
> wet tea bags. ZOT! (giggles and sips again) And there shall rise
> a mighty clacking of dentures, and a tapping of canes... (35)

Peggy's mood of defiant optimism shifts back to her feeling of humiliation and anger, as she thinks about society's conception of her. She has been called an "old prune," (35) an "old girl," and a "senior citizen." (36) Peggy rejects all these labels which debase her individuality. "I am not an object."..."I am me. I am not Josh Murdoch's girl. I am not Herb Woodgreen's wife. I am not Marion Logan's mother. I am me." (36) Peggy refuses to dissolve her identity into the social contents of the patriarchal formula. Buddy echoes religious tradition which advocates the importance of conformity. "It is not good for man to be alone." Peggy herself reads from the Bible about togetherness:

> "Two are better than one; because they have good reward for
> their labour. For if they fall, the one will lift up his fellow: but
> woe to him, that is alone when he falleth; for he hath not
> another to help him up." (37)

110

Peggy is made to feel her existence is deficient because she is alone, and reverberates the biblical claim, "how can one be warm alone?" (37) She remembers the reassurances from others that Herb is still with her in spirit. Buddy echoes this sentiment, "Herb is still with you." To escape from loneliness, Peggy knows she can bring Herb back by evoking "fond memories and warm smiles." However, what she misses most is Herb's physical presence.

Through introspection, Peggy slips back into her younger conscious-ness. She recites Herb's declarations of love, "'til death us do part." (38) The light in the ceiling blows out and Peggy appears as a shadowy figure of her younger self.

> Oh, my love, oh, my love. In the darkness I am always young,
> and still waiting for you. Why did you leave me so soon? I
> miss you. I still miss you. Sometimes at night you come to me.
> I can still remember the little half-smile on your mouth just
> before you came into me, and then I would shut my eyes and
> hold you, rising and arching to the glory of you in me, and
> me all around you. (39)

Like Old Bessie, Peggy reclaims her erotic, vibrant young self. As a Venus figure, she seeks deliverance from the decrepitude of old age by calling forth her dynamic sexual being: active and all-encompassing. However, her old self stoically reminds her of mundane reality. "No dreams and no illusions. And they don't make light bulbs the way they used to." (39) Peggy changes the light bulb and begins to speculate on the inevitability of approaching death. "That is the last time I will change a light bulb. Little by little we leave the world." (39) Her pleasure at having fixed the light is diminished by society's overwhelm-ing impression of old age as synonymous with irrelevance. Peggy echoes the social worker's attitude: "My dear, you can see she's incompetent, can't do for herself at all, you know." (39) Peggy has a comic-tragic vision of nursing homes where the elderly are suffocated with "care." There is the "Bide-a-Wee Home," (40) where they play with marbles and toss bean bags all day; there is "Belly Acres," (41) a peaceful place right next to the cemetery, "controlled by nurses trained in Belsen and doctors skilled in the art of heavy sedation." There is also "Tranquillity Towers," where a "tranc in time saves nine." (41)

Peggy's cynical vision affirms her fight against old age as non-being. However, her consciousness fluctuates between her past memories of hope for the future and her present state of despair. "I used to wonder what the future held for me, lying there all bright and glossy ahead of me. And now—this is the future. There isn't any more where this came from." (42) She tries to cling to the belief that life is still worth living, in spite of Buddy's claim that "there *is* no tomorrow." (42)

Confused by the effects of the sherry, Peggy's identity becomes blurred as she toasts herself: "And to me. Whoever I am." (43) Buddy reminds her of her role as the creator of life, "You are the Mother." (43) Peggy stuffs a pillow up her sweater and proudly displays her pregnancy. "I am the Mother." She mimics the perception of motherhood as "institution,"[15] as her patronizing doctor strips her of power." Now, Mrs. Woodgreen, how are we feeling today? Putting on a little weight, aren't we? We wouldn't want that, would we now?" (43) Peggy re-enacts her birth experience, encouraging herself: "The only way is through." (43)

As Peggy relives the struggle of her pregnancy, the humiliation of the police interrogation overshadows her imagination. The policeman had asked her, "And do you think you'll get pregnant?" (44) As she recalls the cruelty of the police, Peggy's despair becomes intolerable. "I can't stand it any longer. They've spoiled it all, what little I had left, they've spoiled it." (44) In Peggy's state of distress, her instinct for survival is mingled with self-immolation as she represents the double image of life and death. She comforts herself and caresses her pregnant belly, but when she catches a glimpse of herself in the mirror, she is overcome by her deep loathing of her aged image. "You stupid, old fool. You're seventy-two years old, and you're still playing games. When are you going to quit? Right..now!" (44)

Overcome with self-hatred, Peggy tries to force Buddy to kill her with a kitchen knife. However, as much as she wants to die, her instinct to live is stronger and she cannot kill herself. Yet Peggy still longs for liberation from the futility of her life.

> You have to have a reason to get out of bed each morning. And what was my reason today? I was going to vindicate myself today, do my bit for women everywhere, make a stand for justice. It was something to look forward to. I was going to make a little victory of it, a celebration. But they spoilt it. I'm tired of living life to the hilt. I want to die…to the hilt. (46)

The indifference of the outside world has taken away Peggy's faith in human existence. Severed from any form of justice from the legal system, her life seems devoid of meaning.

Buddy, however, articulates her inner consciousness, one that still believes in the power of her existence. He supports her strong conviction that suicide is a sin, and quotes the commandment, "Thou shalt not kill." (47) Peggy grapples with her inner voice, wishing to free herself from her utter disillusionment with mankind and the suffering the world inflicts upon her. In her desperate frenzy, she grabs the knife and begins to stab the puppet, cutting herself in the wrist by accident. This self-mutilation brings her back to her senses, as her life-affirming nature takes over.

> You're going to live, and you're going to keep on living until you are permitted to die. (pause) I have just lost another option of my life. (thinks) I guess it never was an option.

(pause) I won't go brainstorming the gates of eternity again.
I'll wait 'til I'm invited. (48)

Peggy comes to the realization that she must regain meaning in her daily existence, no matter how inadequate it may sometimes appear. She begins to see the trivial details of everyday life as significant again. "Tomorrow I will buy some All-Bran...and maybe a banana." (48) Peggy's new hope and determination is juxtaposed with the taped singing of a nursery rhyme about an old woman leading a life of futility, without control or impact on society.

> ...She'd nothing to lose,
> She'd nothing to fear,
> She'd nothing to ask,
> And nothing to give,
> And when she did die,
> She'd nothing to leave. (48)

Betty Jane Wylie's vision of an old woman's oppression in a hostile urban society is a clear deviation from Hollinsgworth's portrayal of female effacement in the misery of domesticity. Whereas the characters in *Ever Loving* are trapped in their stifling roles as wives and mothers which prevent them from achieving autonomy, Peggy, however, is oppressed through her isolation from others. Her solitude, then, becomes a form of imprisonment in which she is controlled by poverty, fear and loneliness. Where Muriel in *Islands* chooses solitude as a way of liberating herself from human relationships, and Luce in *Ever Loving* leaves her conventional husband in order to fulfill her potential, Peggy's solitude only makes her dream of the past, when she was connected to those she loved and had a meaningful social position as a teacher.

In *The Twisted Loaf*, Bessie struggles in an urban setting to preserve her family tradition, despite the foreign values of urban materialism. Like

Peggy, Bessie experiences the corruption of the outside world and the threat of male violence through rape—in Bessie's case, the rape of her daughter. Like Bessie, Peggy searches for her eternal self in the face of physical deterioration and approaching death. Yet Peggy's greatest obstacle is that she must continue to live in a world which has abandoned her by denying her justice. As an old woman, she perceives a mechanical world ruled by male violence, against which she must struggle alone.

Man's urban reality grew out of the transformation of nature into a technological and mechanical structure. The play portrays the distortion of human behaviour in which violence towards women in the form of rape is symptomatic of man's alienation from his natural being and the world of nature. Peggy withdraws from the corruption of the urban wilderness, by delving into her female inner landscape. Through the medium of her puppet, she escapes into the richness of her imaginary world, keeping at bay the terrors of a living death. She thus creates a tenuous order over the negative forces of the wasteland outside, by drawing sustenance from the natural, human impulses deep within herself.

NOTES

1. Frye. p. 141.
2. Jones, Douglas G. *Butterfly on Rock: A Study of Themes and Images in Canadian Literature*, Toronto: University of Toronto Press, 1970. p. 57.
3. de Beauvoir. p. 180.
4. Griffin, Susan. *Woman and Nature*, New York: Harper and Row, 1978, p. 155.
5. Griffin, Susan. *Rape: The Power of Consciousness*, New York: Harper and Row, 1979, p. 53.
6. Ruether, Rosemary Radford. *Sexism and God-Talk: Toward a Feminist Theology*, Boston: Beacon Press, 1983, p. 263.
7. Singer. p. 313.
8. Ibid. pp. 316-317.
9. Griffin. *Woman and Nature*, pp. 159-160.

10. Atwood. *Survival,* p. 210.
11. Griffin. *Rape,* p. 21.
12. Ibid.
13. de Beauvoir. p. 162.
14. Ibid. pp. 162-163.
15. Rich. p. 13.

VI

La Sagouine

In Antonine Maillet's play, *La Sagouine*, produced in 1971, self-discovery evolves from the margins of French Acadian life. The sense of estrangement experienced by La Sagouine, a poor washerwoman, is mirrored in the displacement of Acadian culture which struggles to exist on the outer edge of New Brunswick society. A non-citizen, the result of her ancestral expulsion by the British in 1755, La Sagouine is the prototypal exile figure. French speaking in an English setting, and a woman in a male-oriented society, the political ramifications of race and gender keep La Sagouine on the perimeter of life. Female oppression in the play is linked to imperial domination of Acadian culture as both the heroine and her native Acadia are symbols of exploitation by colonial rule.

The exile figure in Canadian literature often searches for a way out of alienation and the attainment of integration. This takes the shape of the quest for a lost Paradise, what D.G. Jones sees as the central "archetypal pattern"[1] of Canadian literature. As in the Old Testament, the Canadian Adam is "separated from his Creator and cast out of Eden to wander in the wilderness."[2] Thus the national sense of exile and isolation motivates the Adam figure to regain the lost Utopia, as in Gabrielle Roy's *The Magic Mountain* and Henry Kreisel's *The Betrayal*.

Canadian women playwrights have reinterpreted this search from a female perspective. In *La Sagouine*, Maillet transforms the archetypal pattern of the lost Paradise into the female quest for lost identity. In national terms, the Acadian paradisal state existed prior to the colonial invasion when the Acadian people possessed their land, language and own identity. The desire to restore this former state of glory inspires the modern Acadian imagination.

> They walked for days 'n months through the woods to come back home, cause them also wanned to have a country. They wanned to get 'mselves a patch of land, where they could speak their own language. (167)

In much the same way, La Sagouine is driven to recover a precarious sense of integration. Yet La Sagouine's struggle is more complex than that of the male exile as it includes notions of gender. The historical oppression of women adds a further dimension to La Sagouine's experience of aliena-tion as she must contend with the patriarchal tradition. The banished female figure, unlike the literary Adam, is subjected to domestic hardship and constant child-bearing. As an Eve figure who is responsible for the Fall, La Sagouine has lost her place in the Acadian garden of Eden. A symbol of female punishment for her sins, La Sagouine is shown per-petually scrubbing an endless floor with a bucket of swill.

> Maybe I got a dirty face 'n cracked skin but, Mister, my hands are white! my hands are white 'cause I had 'em in water all my life. Spent my life cleanin. Sure I look dirty, spent my life cleanin other people's dirt. (15)

Her years of hardship as a result of her fall from grace have turned her into a social outcast. The term "La Sagouine" means a "dirty woman engaged in low-status casual labour." However, La Sagouine's hands are always white, a sign of her enduring purity and authenticity despite her misery.

What makes Maillet's work different from her Anglophone contemporaries is her representation of the Catholic Church. Unlike Protestant women of the English tradition, French Canadian women associate patriarchal imperialism with the Catholic religion's domination of women. In *La Sagouine*, the Church is a complex patriarchal structure and the priest is the incarnation of the divine Father who keeps woman in her place.

When matriarchal societies were superseded by the paternalistic model, female myths and imagery were appropriated by the male vision. The Bible, for example, describes how the tree of life and the sea of fresh water were taken away as punishment for Eve's role in the Fall. The imagery of water in *La Sagouine* is both oppressive and regenerative. Water, when used to clean other people's dirt, becomes a form of subjugation, yet her primeval connection with the sea empowers her with a mythological status that transcends limitations. Once associated with female power in the image of the Ocean Mother, the sea is a constant source of inspiration to La Sagouine. It is by the sea that the young La Sagouine discovers love, and the creative energy of the sea unfolds a world of imagination and sensuality. By the sea she comes across a German boy with "sad eyes" who always sings the same song about the deportation of his family. The most life-enhancing expressions, those of compassion and tenderness, are brought forth by the sea. Engulfed by the restorative capacities of the sea, together they attain a spontaneous joy related to self-revelation. The purification of water brings out an innocence and authenticity, as she notices "his hands whiter 'n better kept than that of a lawyer." (28) The sea also plays a part in the transformation of the individual by producing a change in consciousness.

> Ah! wasn' easy, wasn' easy to explain. Seemed to me the sea
> had changed colour. It was a deeper blue than usual, 'n the
> fish was swimmin near the surface of the water like they
> wanned to play with the seagulls. (28)

The sublime powers of the natural world reflect the ebb and flow of La Sagouine's inner nature. Her individual perception is at its most powerful when she describes the grandeur of nature.

La Sagouine's monologue is an awakening of consciousness from the silent darkness below. Written in the Acadian dialect, the play gives impetus to a woman with a unique language and oral tradition. The role of language in the play is related to the rediscovery of Acadian origins and returns to "original sources,"[3] a language that is rooted in "the body and the earth."[4] For according to French feminists like Chantal Chawaf, the female artist's creativity comes out of the gaps and margins of history. Rising from the substratum, it "stirs up our sensuality, wakes it up, pulls it away from indifferent inertia."[5] The Acadian dialect in the play represents the articulation of female identity, as mother tongue is linked to ancient origins and the retracing of a forgotten vision. La Sagouine's dialogue is an expression of emotional and personal experience which she brings into the world of theatre. Like the mothers throughout history who told their children fairy-tales, the female oral tradition unites women with a meaningful past. Maillet's deliberate use of Acadian dialect, a French similar to that spoken in the 17th century, reminds Acadians of the importance of their heritage prior to the Deportation when their culture flourished. The retrieval of this forgotten language touches primordial roots, with woman as the primeval creator of life. La Sagouine, as the Mother of Creation, uses drama as a means of revealing a neglected cultural expression and a silenced female voice. La Sagouine's vision brings both cultures out of obscurity.

The play returns to the preadamite origins of drama, when drama took the form of fertility rituals with woman as both priestess and creator. Women's ancient connection with drama further impels the rediscovery of a feminist consciousness as women playwrights search for the inchoation of female creativity.

> ...the origins of female consciousness, to learn if something sacred, which was lost, still lives, and if the work of women

in theatre has been impelled and shaped by remembrance of a time when women were sanctioned to create.[6]

The theatrical imagination of La Sagouine expresses a richness that is spontaneous; embedded in the earth itself. Through her imagination she is able to transcend the drudgery of her position as a washerwoman and gain a sense of power lacking in her own life. It is through art, particularly the art of parody, that La Sagouine achieves dignity and a sense of control over her situation. Through her monologue she becomes an empowered woman, and like an ancient fertility Goddess, expounds her vision before a social gathering. Yet it is only through this theatrical discourse that La Sagouine can affirm her individuality, and, mop in hand, she is at once a symbol of female creativity taking centre stage and a symbol of female oppression forced to clean "other people's dirt."

Like the protagonists in *The Twisted Loaf* and *A Place on Earth*, La Sagouine's speech becomes an artistic reordering of experience which weaves through the heroine's inner consciousness, shifting from the past to the present in an attempt to achieve a recognition of self. Throughout her monologue, she infuses her world with myth and creativity, elevating herself out of oppression. Like Peggy in *A Place on Earth*, La Sagouine's vision discloses a secret world separate from male experience. Both protagonists must battle against poverty and old age in defining their individuality.

La Sagouine is reminiscent of Old Bessie in *The Twisted Loaf* who, as a Jew in a gentile world, is also ghettoized by race, language and gender. But La Sagouine's plight is even more tragic than Bessie's, for not only does she epitomize the estranged exile, she is also denied Acadian citizenship.

Gender plays a further role in limiting her options in society: She can either marry, become a "fille du joie," or a cleaning woman. Her marriage to Gapi, a poor fisherman, only increases her oppression as he does nothing "apart fr'm bein grouchy." Marriage did not bring her the promised economic security, and she finds herself having to support the whole family. Unlike most men who support their families, La Sagouine is denied the power of the bread winner and is still responsible for the domestic duties at home. La Sagouine's marriage to Gapi mirrors her relationship with God as both possess the power to rule over her. Yet her apparent submission to their power is merely for the sake of convention, for in her private world she challenges both her husband and her patriarchal God.

Although her cleaning job gets her out of the house, it does not give her a place in her community. While she is young enough, she prostitutes herself in secret, going into town to meet men. In the patriarchal tradition, the prostitute is the perennial fallen woman, the Mary Magdalen in religious imagery. The Mary Magdalen figure in religious terms is the reformed seductress who becomes a symbol of mystical contemplation, thus transforming her sensual, physical nature into a divine image of religious purity. In the feminist vision, both Eve and Mary Magdalen reflect aspects of the original female archetype, the Mother Goddess. As a prostitute, La Sagouine is the evil seductress of religious imagery, and through her bond with nature, is also the life-affirming woman of goddess imagery. Losing her position as a "fille de joie" signals the end of her youth and erotic power. With her fading beauty comes the drabness of life as a washerwoman. She relates this fall from grace to a form of exile in which she loses her sense of place.

> At first I didn' have to exile myself to get by. Could stay in these parts; they was enough work between le Russeau des Pottes 'n la Butte du Moulin. But when you start gettin older, bit by bit you gotta let go some territory, cause you ain't the only one to make a livin. (29)

This isolation includes a world without love, for society denies her the experience of love by imprisoning her German lover during the war. The sea reflects this loss of love and absence of wonder. "Right then'n there, seems the sea changed colour, 'n even the seagulls never cried like they did before." (29)

Although La Sagouine feels the oppression of her low status job, she is able to surmount the drabness of her chores by recounting tales about her life. She goes beyond mere storytelling by displaying the moral corruption of the powers that rule: the government, the Catholic Church, and the rich. Her humour adds intelligence and grace to her observations, giving her a dignity she lacks in her routine existence. Her accounts deal largely with the Catholic Church which has been instrumental in keeping the Acadians oppressed. In sections like "The Christmas," "The Priests" and "The Good Lord is Good," La Sagouine depicts the hypocrisy and corruption of Christianity which has turned religion into a hierarchical power struggle, far from the celebration of a humble saviour's birth. For Christ, she reminds us, was born in a barn without the luxury and comforts of the rich. The Christ in the Christmas show at church is a pampered imposter, wrapped in a silk blanket, far removed from reality. The exclusive mentality of the Church makes religion out of reach for those at the bottom of the social ladder.

> ...didn' stink like sheep'n have a barn smell in there. We was the only ones that didn' smell good in the whole church, that's how come we stayed in the back. Didn' have no frilly clothes, none of us, 'n no curly hair. We wouldn' of dared to stand even beside the shepherds, better believe it! (41)

La Sagouine and her poor neighbours are in fact closer to the authentic figure of Jesus, who, like them, was born in a shed surrounded by animal smells. In their houses "the manure was fer real. I'm telling you, 'n so was the straw." (42) By referring to the animal odours, she speaks for the physical world which is absent from the Church's unearthly religion.

La Sagouine points to the priests' distorted perception of the human condition. Cleaning away the dirt and alleviating smells is associated with the priests' contempt for the body and the natural process, the patriarchal

"alienation from nature,"[7] like the priests who live in sterilized surroundings far removed from life.

> Wasn' use' to our smell, the poor souls, they lived in their nice
> rectories scrubbed clean all year long, where it would only
> smell of Bon Ami 'n Lemon Oil. A priest jus' wasn' use' to our
> dirt. (72)

The play also expresses the Church's desire to control and classify,
exemplified by the congregation's obsession to purchase pews at the front of
the church, a sign of social superiority. By describing the war zone created by
a dispute over a couple of pews, Maillet conveys the absurdity of territorial
rights and the Church's need to claim possession and power. From this
standpoint, religion becomes a weapon with which to subjugate others.

> The front pews are fer'em folks in fur coats 'n silkscarfs; 'n
> those that come to church wearin mackinaws 'n gumrubbers,
> well, they gotta be happy with the chairs in the back; 'n us, we
> gotta stand on our own two feet, like we always did. (98)

La Sagouine's sense of irony often takes on a tone of defiance against
the patriarchal Catholic Church. In "The Good Lord is Good" section, La
Sagouine rebels against religious control by demanding the priests justify
their power over others.

> Ah! yep, we'll ask 'em there to tell us everythin:what's okay,
> what's a no-no; where it's okay 'n not okay; 'n how come the
> same things ain't no-nos to everybody; 'n what makes the
> priest decide to forbid one thing instead of the other. (122)

As a woman she questions the sexist attitudes of the bishop and
perceives his pretence of virtue as a disguise for his dislike of women. She

bluntly cuts through the philosophical dogma which holds women responsible for the Fall of Man. La Sagouine wonders how one priest she knew could distrust "his own mother," when she was burdened with 18 children. She refers to the victimization of women who are still despised by the priesthood even though they have been stripped of power.

> Ah! a woman is always a woman, the bishop use' to say. 'n she's the one that committed the first sin in the Garden of Eden. Her man took a bite off the apple only cause his wife gave it to him. (124)

This is why the bishop believes women must be punished and should "obey her man who's the boss 'n the strongest." She challenges this fallacy by pointing out the inconsistency in the argument: "A man is only weak when he's tempted by his wife, apart fr'm that, he's always the strongest."

In her discussion of the Fall of Eve, La Sagouine makes reference to life prior to the Fall and why any woman would sacrifice her freedom so easily—for a life of struggle and pain. Her own theory is that Eve was pushed into eating the apple, for no woman would be stupid enough to give up her Paradise for a single apple, "no matter how juicy it is." She alludes to a possible conspiracy—that women did not cause their own fall but were forced into it. "…someone pushed her; 'r else it was a trap; 'r that it had to happen so that we could earn back our heaven by the sweat of our brow." The myth of the Fall has been interpreted by feminist thinkers as a patriarchal creation designed to justify the appropriation of female power and the subsequent domination over women. In feminist terms, the Fall from Paradise signifies woman's separation from the natural world and the estrangement from her own body which was once a divine manifestation of all creation.

Retrieving a lost Utopia in *La Sagouine* mirrors the protagonist's search for self-recognition, for the absence of harmony parallels the loss of individuality and freedom. La Sagouine is no longer free to live on impulse but must comply with authoritarian rules and structures which seem absurd to her. Yet through the richness of her inner world she maintains a little piece of Paradise whereby she expands the boundaries set by society. From another dimension, Paradise is an image representing La Sagouine's unrealized potential. This inner landscape fosters her intrinsic self free from social conformity.

La Sagouine's view of the paradisal state is firmly rooted in the physical world. A comfortable house is the materialization of her personal need for harmony; her refuge from the suffering of the outside world. She sees the irony of liberated women who are dissatisfied with being in the house and want to get out, when all she wants is the chance to be inside.

> Jus' when they have everythin inside, that's when they wanna leave. Maybe that's what would of happened to me too, hard to say! I reckon a person gets bored of everythin. Even of feelin good. (136)

La Sagouine humourously has a cure for anyone bored of feeling good— they could always come over to her shack and wash clothes outside in subzero temperatures, "'n eat warmed up beans 'n pancakes" every day.

La Sagouine's wish for harmony makes her remember the joys of the past which is always the rebirth of spring in her memory. While she still believes in dreams and a Heaven on Earth, Gapi represents the loss of dreams and innocence. His cynicism about the government and the Church gives him a contempt for life, even for the arrival of spring. La Sagouine, on the other hand, still has the ability to feel joy and remembers the happy moments of her life. She finds humour in his defiant anger. "Gapi says he don't want nobody's help; well, that's cause he knows even if he wanned some, he wouldn' get none...Ain't easy. (143) Although she sees Gapi as a broken man, in her imagination she conjures up the young man she used to know, infusing vitality and life into his broken frame. "Young 'n sturdy, he was, 'n his shoulders was stronger than a moose, that's right!" (143) She associates his vibrancy with the spring and the rebirth of the natural cycle, when the seagulls were coming back from the South and the sap was dripping from the branches.

The natural world in the play is linked to La Sagouine's well-being as the spring stirs the life force lying dormant within her. She describes the physical connection with the earth in which the human body takes on nature's form.

> Our skin is kind of brown 'n a little bit cracked; 'n as we grow ol', the wrinkles of the face look like furrows in a garden; 'n bones get crooked at the joints like branches of a birch tree; 'n feet sink into the earth like they wanned to take root. We look like this land, I'm telling you. (145)

Nature gives her sustenance and the strength to overcome her oppression. For La Sagouine, both the land and sea take on female characteristics and as Mother Earth, restore and nurture those who inhabit her world.

> This land, 'n the sea. She's the one that fed us most 'n saved us fr'm distress. When the land happens to fail you, you still got the sea, with its clams 'n its smelts. Shouldn' speak ill of the sea, I says to the others, she saved us so many many times. Even if high tides in Fall come 'n get you right up to yer kitchen floor; 'n the ice in Spring takes yer boat at sea; 'n storms on the other side of the sand dunes drown fishermen every year. Even then, she's the one that made us, 'n looks like us the most. (145)

The sea, with its ability to create life and death, has omnipotent powers which must be respected. She supplies the nourishment which gives us life but she can also destroy those who do not understand her power. This entails more than trying to exploit her resources, but by identifying with her existence, and assuming her characteristics.

Usin her as a mirror, our eyes turned deep 'n blue, 'n havin watched so long fer fish deep in the water, our cheeks rose high 'n our brows grew close. (146)

Through this connection with the sea we recognize our natural beings. The sea becomes a reflection of our own existence in which we see our deeper selves. The sea also has the ability to transform us, awaken our senses and shape our awareness. With the vitality of nature exists the potential for human growth.

As an archetype in the female consciousness, the matriarchal association with nature gives historical significance to the modern desire for self-discovery. For La Sagouine, the memory of completeness is triggered by the sea and the rebirth of spring. When spring comes she recalls the power of the natural cycle and her primeval link with the changing seasons, which produces "an achin fer the sun...way back then." (147) The power of recollection restores her higher self, separate from the domestic hardship of her daily life. Nature stimulates her deepest memory and brings her to the enlightenment of being.

...you see wild geese passin over 'n goin inland, behind yer father's place, right where you was born 'n where you was raised. 'n you see a drop of water clingin to the tip of a branch, 'n then you hear it fall on the snow, 'n run in the furrow, 'n rush to the shore, into the sea. 'n you can jus' feel the clover that'd like to come out of the earth, 'n the ice goin down the river. 'n the seagulls cryin after the wild geese, 'n the wild geese still flyin north...'n you don't know where you are no more. (147-148)

La Sagouine's sensitivity to the awakening world around her is experienced as a religious revelation. She awakens out of her domestic cocoon and begins to feel the energy rush through her veins. She witnesses for this fleeting moment the immanence of her being and the essence of life itself. This is her moment of Paradise regained; her integration with self and place. She wishes to merge completely with this omnipotent life force, yet she realizes she is still restrained.

> All yer memories, all yer hopes, 'n all yer achin. You feel like whistlin, 'n diddlin... but you can't cause you got that cork right here 'n cotton-wool where the lungs is... (148)

Her sense of integration is incomplete, marred by the external limitations imposed upon her. However, her consciousness has been affected by the experience and she remains transformed. The experience with nature has a religious dimension which transports her to a higher plane. Her burdens weigh heavily upon her, yet the splendour remains enshrined in her imagination. She envisions a time when this happiness would be immutable; a spring that lasts forever. This she calls "Paradise."

> But one day, maybe we'll find a Spring season, a real one, drippin all over 'n reekin of musk, with endless processions of wild geese in the sky, 'n no more achin, just a nice easy feelin in yer throat 'n all over the skin, a real Spring that'll never end, but that'll last,... (148)

However, this dream is suffused with an acceptance of the way of the world as she realizes that complete happiness on earth is ephemeral. Unlike her spontaneous connection with nature, the Christian concept of resurrection and afterlife begins to appear as confusing and inconsistent. She sees the fabricated Heaven of the male Church as consisting of rules and obligations, unlike the immediate Paradise of her natural world. "All that holy stuff, it ain't a job fer me." (151) Yet she has been conditioned to believe that the Church's version of Heaven is the accepted form. With a sense of irony, she describes the illogicality of God's divine plan.

> But that don't mean there's som'n wrong with His mind, jus' cause we can't und'stand it. Maybe without'em high tides that year, we wouldn' have any smelts the next one. 'n without depression 'r financial crash, we wouldn' of had soup 'n stamps. 'n would we have had our widow's compensation if our men hadn' died at war? (152)

La Sagouine thinks of God's design of the world and how He could have created it differently. In contrast, she imagines how she might have made the world in her own image. Fundamental to her reinterpretation of Creation is the need to make sense out of a confusing religion, for she has been taught not to question, but to accept blindly. "...the only thing they taught us, it's that a mystery is a truth that you gotta believe in, but that you don't und'stand." (155) The priests and the lawyers, on the other hand, have the education needed to understand. They also have the power to keep people in the shadow of ignorance, for the patriarchal hierarchy is based on the inferiority of others. Women have been prevented from understanding God, just as they have been denied intellectual analysis. God, made to represent "the Word,"[8] is the historical language of the male intellect barred to women. Without this freedom to scrutinize the nature of God, women remained trapped within a socio-political order in which they had no part in developing.

Denied the language of inquiry, La Sagouine speaks from the illiterate margins with the voice of subversion. Her direct honesty comes from underground and penetrates the censored gaps in women's history. She presents a vision of the world that is fragmented and incomplete because it has excluded the experience of women. Through her monologue, La Sagouine breaks the silence. Her words come out of the crevices of the dark earth, animating the muted voices of the past. And like her Acadian culture, her vision, despite the threat of assimilation, still lives.

La Sagouine's final judgment calls for the transformation of religious dogma into a celebration of life. She envisions a religion based on human experience; a life-enhancing ritual rooted in the moment.

> Ain't askin fer castles, or Californias, or plastic flowers. But if the angels could whip up a wild-duck stew 'n a store-bought coconut pie, n' if our Father-in-Heaven in person could come around 'n call the dance on Saturday nights, we wouldn' mind it. Fer a Paradise like that one, we wouldn' whine so much about death...wouldn' be afraid any more...we'd croak happy, My God, yes!... (182-183)

La Sagouine's depiction of religion reclaims the abandoned physical world and becomes a fertile ground for human fulfillment.

La Sagouine is both an affirmation of Acadian culture which has been undermined by mainstream Canadian society, and the assertion of the unacknowledged female voice in the patrilineal structure. The experience of abandonment unites the Acadian quest for recognition in an alien land with the feminist validation of women in a man's world. La Sagouine frees her imprisoned history from the paralysis of silence, and with a bold eloquence and endearing charm, demands that we listen.

NOTES

1. Jones. p. 15.
2. Ibid.
3. Chawaf, Chantal. "Linguistic Flesh," *New French Feminisms: An Anthology,* Elaine Marks and Isabelle de Courtivron. Eds. Amherst: University of Massachusetts Press, 1980. p. 177.

4. Ibid.
5. Ibid.
6. Malpede. p. 2.
7. Ruether, p.71.
8. Chopp, Rebecca S. *The Power to Speak: Feminism, Language, God.* New York: Cross Road Publishing, 1989, p. 3.

VII

A Woman From the Sea

In Cindy Cowan's play, *A Woman From the Sea*, produced in 1986, the creative potential offered by the wilderness takes on new significance. Where the wilderness in *Ever Loving* symbolizes patriarchal society, and becomes a place of refuge in *Islands* and *La Sagouine*, the wilderness in *A Woman From the Sea* is used as a metonym for the female life process. The "Nature as Woman" motif in Canadian writing reaches new heights as both nature and woman are portrayed as the affirmation of life in the face of technological destruction. Whilst the wilderness in Canadian literature has often been perceived as hostile to man, demonstrating a "mindless barbarity,"[1] in *A Woman From the Sea*, it is the hostility of man that threatens to annihilate the natural world. Northrop Frye sees this shift of consciousness occurring in "the second phase of Canadian social development,"[2] when man's technological atrocities have managed to subdue the forces of nature and the individual begins to ally himself with the natural world.

> In this version nature, though still full of awfulness and mystery, is the visible representative of an order that man has violated, a spiritual unity that the intellect murders to dissect.[3]

As in Maillet's *La Sagouine* and Atwood's *Surfacing*, in *A Woman From the Sea*, Cindy Cowan modifies the literary prototype by associating the lost

Paradise with the matriarchal "Golden Age." The female loss of identity becomes the struggle to regain the ancient correlation with nature in pre-patriarchal society, "when Goddess-worship prevailed, and when myths depicted strong and revered female figures."[4] Man's search for integration with the natural world is thus reshaped into a female mythology whereby the primeval religion of the Mother Goddess symbolizes all existence. The image of the Goddess has become a symbol for the restoration of female authenticity in the feminist imagination, as Carol P. Christ demonstrates:

> The image of the Goddess that is reemerging in the psyches
> of modern women is symbolic of women's sense that the
> power we are claiming for ourselves through the women's
> movement is rooted in the ground of being itself.[5]

In Cowan's play, the connection with the natural process is attained through female fertility. The protagonist, Almira, gains a deeper awareness of nature through becoming pregnant, and discovering the psychic energy of her being. Motherhood for the playwright symbolizes both the life cycle and the creative process, as Cindy Cowan was inspired to write the play after giving birth to her child.

> As I lifted my eyes to the sea that forever surrounds me in
> Nova Scotia I started to hear a story. One of destruction and
> birth and the endurance and power of women's love. A love
> which must be far greater than the megatons of destruction
> released by a single nuclear explosion.[6]

Giving birth exemplifies the female correspondence with nature, life, and creative energy. Cindy Cowan explores her metaphysical connection with the natural world inspired by her own experience of motherhood and creativity. "Lying on the table, between my shaking legs, was a living human being. This was power. Real power! Like the wind and water and fire."[7]

As in *La Sagouine,* the play reaffirms women's ancient relationship with theatre and ritual. Women's central role at seasonal rituals like that of Eleusis and Thesmophoria of ancient Greece gave birth to the art of drama through the worship of female fertility, thereby achieving archetypal status in the modern quest for female artistic identity.

> In each and every one of these life-desiring, life-affirming rituals which are the origins of drama, women played major roles as characters, performers, and creators, as the ones who imagined the content and who wrought the form.[8]

Playwright Cindy Cowan explores the dramatic link between female mythology and the primeval forces of nature in the setting of the Nova Scotia seashore. Described as a "fourth character"[9] in the play, the natural environment of the seashore becomes a dynamic Supreme Being. The sound of the sea and the music in the play give expression to the forces of nature and add emphasis to the emotional process of the three characters, Sedna, Almira, and George.

The protagonist, Almira, like Muriel in *Islands,* leaves the corruption of society in pursuit of individual meaning. However, it is Almira's husband, George, who brings her to the deserted Nova Scotian coast to enjoy the splendour of the unspoilt landscape. Almira herself has become cynical and disillusioned, seeing the cabin he brings her to as a "fish shack," one that is ridden with "feathers and mouse droppings." (65) George tries to awaken Almira to the beauty of the scenery, but Almira remains unstirred. Involved in the fight against the seal hunt, they have come to observe the behaviour of seals. But Almira feels her efforts to prevent the seal hunt have been in vain and begins to withdraw from the natural world. Almira's despair signifies her disconnection from her environment. Because of her inner turmoil, she is unable to retrieve a connection with her exterior world.

The mythical Inuit sea creature, Sedna—half seal and half human, serves to link mankind with the natural world and to the inner process of Almira's character. The 'boom' sounds in the play represent the powerful presence of Sedna, as well as "the disintegration of Almira's grasp on reality."[10] Sedna is able to change from woman to seal at will. Like La Sagouine she is also a symbol of the female link with the primeval past, reflecting the richness of imagination; one that correlates with the natural world through ritual and mythology. As an image of the "Lady of the Animals,"[11] depicted in the cave drawings and figurines of Paleolithic and Neolithic times, Sedna is a personification of humanity's earliest imaginative consciousness, expressing the "image of the awesome creative power of woman and nature."[12]

The desire to retrieve the lost alliance between humankind and nature is a prominent theme in the Canadian imagination, typified by works like Marian Engel's novel *Bear* and Ringwood's plays *The Deep Has Many Voices* and *The Lodge*. Frye perceives the search for the lost connection with nature in the form of the pastoral myth as "the most explicitly mythopoeic aspect of Canadian literature."[3] As part of the pastoral myth and the "vision of vanished grandeur,"[14] Cindy Cowan's interpretation of the myth explores the atrophied state of the relationship between female creation and nature. As a representation of the natural process, Sedna tries to reunite Almira with the primeval life force. She chooses Almira, a lost and confused woman, as her medium for the communication of natural powers. As if her subconscious is being awakened by a forgotten dream, Almira responds when Sedna calls her name, reminding her of her inner self and the natural world from which she has severed herself.

George is the first to meet Sedna on the beach, hoping to sight a Hood seal. Sedna appears as a wise old woman who tells George her father was a fisherman and once saw a strange sea creature that waved at him. George goes back to the cabin full of the excitement and magic of the sea only to be met with Almira's scepticism. "Something out of a bottle of Hermits." (67) Almira takes the binoculars and stares out to sea in a trance-like state, singing the words to an old seal hunting song, "Death to our best friends," (67) having never heard it before. George notices a change is taking place within Almira's perception, but he is unsure of what it means. Almira unconsciously is beginning to incorporate Sedna into her being, but her thoughts are fragmented and her focus is scattered. As a result of her separation from nature, Almira lunches on processed food like pink popcorn and chips, unconcerned about the effects on her body. "What's the point in being healthy?" (69)

George, on the other hand, believes eating well and exercising is an important form of discipline. "Combat discipline. To fight the enemy." (69) He deals with reality in practical terms and sees Almira as over-emotional and "melodramatic." (70) He is intent on preventing the hunting of seals by climbing onto the ice floes to save their lives, unlike Almira who once saw the importance of pressuring the government towards protection. In her disillusionment over the failure of protecting seals, Almira declares she is "retreating from society." (70) George is alarmed by Almira's ability to give up caring, but she insists that "Not caring feels very, very good." At this point, the sound of the boom is heard, signalling Sedna's arrival. It is followed by a terrible smell, "Like something dead," (71) observes Almira. The fact that only Almira smells the odour signifies her awakening consciousness, infused by the presence of Sedna. George is uneasy by what he perceives as Almira's mental disintegration and decides to let her rest.

Sedna appears to George on the beach as a rotting seal corpse which he struggles to push back to sea. In contrast, the life process, emanating through the baying of seals increases in power.

Sedna then enters Almira's dream state, intensifying Almira's nightmare as she rolls up the beach crying in pain. She beckons Almira to look at her and describes the "Thick, crimson blood." (71) Almira tries to avoid facing animal suffering by looking away, but Sedna forces her to experience the horrors of killing. Almira is suddenly woken by George in the middle of her nightmare. "I was drowning. Down...down...down." (71) He tries to reassure her that he got rid of the corpse and the smell of death. But Almira knows that the smell will not go away as the rotting corpse is really herself. "It's me. It's me. It's me..." (72)

By identifying with the destruction of the animal world through her bond with Sedna, Almira begins to associate herself with the exploitation of nature. Frye discusses the "prevalence in Canada of animal stories, in which animals are closely assimilated to human behaviour and emotions."[15] The identification with the animal world by writers like Grey Owl, Farley Mowat, and Margaret Atwood illustrates the search for man's primeval instincts which have been defiled by the corruption of civilization. The destruction of the natural world mirrors man's own self-annihilation. "By devastating nature, man loses his own humanity."[16] Allison Mitcham also reflects this perception when she writes:

> The destruction of our wild animals...ultimately signals our own destruction, for without the wild life our northland indeed becomes the barren wilderness that so many urban dwellers have long, and hitherto falsely, considered it to be.[17]

By relating to the extermination of the seals, like the hanged heron the protagonist identifies with in *Surfacing*, Almira recognizes her own sense of helpless non-being. George tries in vain to reanimate her enthusiasm for the seal campaign, and reads one of the postcards they composed describing the slaughter of the seals. But Almira is disillusioned, saying, "They don't care." (72) She refers to the British government who boycotts Canadian fish to end the seal hunt, but at the same time, "they support the slaughter of sea turtles for a bloody bowl of soup!"

The destruction of the natural world by international governments derives from what Jones sees as western culture's need to bind nature "in the body politic by force of law."[18] By molding nature into a product for consumption, western man is able to assert his rational superiority over the "irrational" physical elements.

> Rather than accept the world as it is, western man has sought
> to transform it, to refashion the world in the image of his
> ideal. Certainly he has enlarged his understanding of nature
> to an astonishing degree, but more often than not he has used
> this understanding to consolidate his power over nature
> rather than to extend his communion with her. He has persist-
> ed in opposing to nature the world of ideas, the world of his
> ideal, and in his idealism he has tended to become exclusive
> rather than inclusive, arrogant rather than humble...[19]

As an expression of this "inclusive" thinking, George, although he
works to save nature, proceeds from the idealism of his intellect when he
plans to fight the seal hunt. "It is very important, at this time, that the
federal government be aware of the desire." (73) Almira, on the other hand,
indicates her need for an emotional involvement with nature. "Desire?"
She has "forgotten desire." George is not concerned with a spontaneous,
emotional association with nature, and rather, imposes his rational consciousness on nature, confidently believing that this year could be the end
of the seal hunt. The boom is heard, and Almira reveals her fear of
annihilation. "I see the end." (73)

The play echoes Atwood's claim that the Canadian identification with
the destruction of the animal world is manifested in the national fear of
extinction, as well as the individual fear of lost identity.

> ...Canadians themselves feel threatened and nearly extinct
> as a nation, and suffer also from life-denying experience as
> individuals—the culture threatens the "animal" within
> them—and that their identification with animals is the ex-
> pression of a deep-seated cultural fear.[20]

Thus Almira's loss of individuality interconnects with the violation of the
animal world. Her identification with animal suffering embodies her own

helpless position in the technological nuclear age which threatens human existence, a recurring theme in the Canadian consciousness, as Atwood discerns.

> ...the English Canadian projects himself through his animal images as a threatened victim, confronted by a superior alien technology against which he feels powerless, unable to take any positive defensive action, and, survive each crisis as he may, ultimately doomed.[21]

By becoming defeated by man's rejection of nature, Almira has allowed man's exploitation to destroy her alliance with the Earth Mother. The 'boom' signifies the presence of Sedna who reminds Almira of her responsibility to the natural world. "You have forgotten our bond." (73) When George talks about leaving the animals in peace, Almira crosses herself "In nomini patri, et filii, et spiritu sanctu." Sedna interprets this from the female perspective, urging Almira to exchange her male-oriented perception for a female-centred vision. "In the name of the mother, the daughter, and the Holy Ghost." (73)

George instigates his plans in an orderly fashion, but Almira can no longer distance herself, becoming overwhelmed with animal suffering. She sympathizes with the helpless pregnant turtles who "lumber up onto the beach to lay their eggs..." (74) They become victims of the male hunters who "hack off their belly plates," and leave them mutilated to die on the beach. George thinks her behaviour is caused by over-work. "You got too close that's all. You need a break." Through her anguish, Almira perceives the decimation of the animal world as the victimization of the female species, for the nesting female becomes the easiest prey. "Listen to me! The seals slaughtered on the ice floes? Nesting females! The annihilation of the penguins, gannets, spearbills, swiftwings...How was it accomplished?" (74)

Cindy Cowan implies that the destruction of animals was accomplished through the separation of human consciousness from nature, restating Ruether's claim that man, by perceiving nature as a product for consumption, uses his "rational knowledge"[22] to manipulate nature. Through the "hierarchical chain of being and chain of command,"[23] man's superior status gives him the power to exploit all other life forms.

> The domination of nature is seen as a system of infinite expansion. The eschatological flight from the finite to the infinite has been turned on its side and converted into a doctrine of infinite progress, as both rational knowledge of and control over nature. Nature is to be impelled forward in infinite expansion of material productivity, and its limits are to be gradually conquered.[24]

Almira, aware of nature's equivocal existence in the nuclear age, sees nature as "fragile." (76) George, on the other hand, perceives nature as "subtle." In his defense he proclaims the life process as continuous since people are still having babies. Almira thinks it is unnatural to have children, as life hinges on the edge of oblivion. Sedna echoes Almira's words and her perception: "Life doesn't seem natural." (77) And in her state of despair Almira believes she would be a "terrible mother."

Almira ruminates upon the distortion of life and hears the boom of nuclear devastation looming in the distance. She begins to see the absurdity of modern life in the technological age. "After the successful explosion of the first atomic bomb, the National Baby Association named Robert Oppenheimer its 'Father of the Year.'" (77) Sedna questions the corruption of the natural process. "If he was the father and the bomb was his baby...who was the mother?" Almira remembers the first mother: Eve. Both Almira and Sedna propound the power of female fertility, envisioning Eve as a dynamic producer of life. George, as the voice of patriarchal tradition, denies the image of Eve as a figure of fertility and power.

ALMIRA: Eve was pregnant.

GEORGE: Almira! She was not.

ALMIRA: Eve ate from the tree of knowledge and put two and two together. She produced life!

SEDNA: Eve rejoiced more for the coming of her child than all the trappings of Paradise!

GEORGE: She didn't. (78)

By perceiving Eve as a fertility figure, Cindy Cowan connects Eve with the Mother Goddess, as does Millett when she describes Eve as a "fertility goddess overthrown."[25]

The 'boom' sound in the play crescendos into a slow explosion, reminding Almira of the inevitable destruction of the apocalyptic myth. "The knowledge of life required the knowledge of death." (78) But in the nuclear age natural life and death have become contorted by a mechanical, artificial process.

> There'll be no more babies. Woman won't be able to have them. We'll keep getting bigger and rounder only there's nothing inside. Nothing! Only some grey mushrooming gas that bloats us. But there can be no baby... (78)

Almira articulates the deformation of the life process through the threat of nuclear destruction; the sole production of man. Technological control and nuclear devastation is an outcome of man's subjugation of nature and the world of instinct. Man is the inimical threat to the survival of the natural environment. "Every human being including myself is my enemy." (78)

George, on the other hand, echoes the conventional idea of motherhood and the family, repeating his mother's words. "A baby brings love into the world." (78) But to Almira this perception seems out of place in the nuclear age. The whole concept of traditional male-female bonding in order to produce a child seems futile to her in the face of an atomic wasteland. George fails to see how the nuclear age has changed the natural order of life. He continues to perceive the creation of life and the demonstration of love as unchanged. Almira, on the other hand, sees everything as fragmented, like her own psyche. "I just want to keep dissolving." (79) George tries to awaken her sensuality and female desires. "You're in a body that's healthy, and round, and soft." He lowers her to the ground and she passively resigns herself to her own oblivion: "Leaden lovers living love lower me to my grave." Again George reiterates the traditional role of his mother. "A baby brings love into the world..." Sedna prevents the love-making from occurring by placing a "musket ball" near Almira. She is overcome by the horror of the recurring odour, but again, George is unable to smell it. Sedna takes the musket ball away and returns to the beach, confirming: "It stinks of fear." (80)

Almira goes down to the beach to dig for clams where she meets Sedna for the first time. At this stage Almira is still resisting unification with the life process. Almira believes she is hallucinating and that she is talking to herself when Sedna reveals she lives "In the mother of us all. She who embraces us, bathes us, and to whom we will return when our time is come...The sea!" (82) The sea is described as a mother image of fertility and nurture, and reverberates the feminist belief that women must reclaim their link with the archetypal primeval past, as Griffin writes,

> Like the sunlight trapped in the leaf which becomes part of
> the ground, of the sea, the body of the fish, body of animal,
> soil, seed. What is growing inside and will pierce the surface,
> if she awakens with this memory: what she was before.[26]

Almira realizes Sedna's words are part of her dream. She is frightened by Sedna's intrusion into her inner consciousness and wants to go back to her state of inertia. But Sedna is determined that Almira acknowledge the destruction of the natural environment. Sedna will leave her alone when "you decide to leave the Earth alone." (84) Both Sedna and Almira share the same consciousness as Almira describes her dream of living in the sea, which dissolves into Sedna's nightmarish vision of animal extermination. Both Sedna and Almira embrace the beauty of the natural world against the opposing threat of man the hunter, the "black silhouettes shimmering in the glare of the ice." (84) The sounds of the crying seals are heard in the distance, as Almira imagines the horror of the attack. "Red! Blood! In my eyes. All around me...thuck...thuck...thuck..." (85) Sedna articulates her betrayal by the patriarchal Father who instituted the subjection of female power by sacrificing her to the sea.

The play expounds the concept that man imposes his will on both woman and nature in order to exorcise his fear of the irrational and instinctive.

> Man seeks in woman the Other as Nature and as his fellow being. But we know what ambivalent feelings Nature inspires in man. He exploits her, but she crushes him, he is born of her and dies in her; she is the source of his being and the realm that he subjugates to his will; Nature is a vein of gross material in which the soul is imprisoned, and she is the supreme reality; she is contingence and Idea, the finite and the whole; she is what opposes the Spirit, and the Spirit itself.[27]

Sedna defies the patriarchal Father who initiated her downfall. "I was your daughter, father."..."Why did you throw me away? I loved you..." (85) The Biblical connotations of Sedna's banishment portray her as an Eve figure, cast out of the garden of Eden by her angry Patriarch and condemned to aimless wandering in the wilderness. Jones sees the ostracism of Eve as a denial of the Divine Mother by patriarchy. "It is that world conventionally symbolized by Eve, the world of the instinctive life, of passion, feeling, and intuition."[28] It is "traditional [patriarchal] culture that leads to the rejection of Eve, the land or mother nature herself."[29] Sedna's exile is interwoven with Almira's sense of betrayal by the bureaucratic male government because she is unable to propel them into action against the seal hunt. "I can do nothing...I've tried." (85) Sedna understands Almira's state of despair, conscious of her own tenuous existence which is constantly being threatened.

By dominating both women and the natural world, man tries to gain control over the life and death process that engulfs him. By the "dictatorship of mind"[30] over "all non-rational life,"[31] man tries to extricate himself from nature's terrifying omnipotence. By subduing nature and woman to his will, man tries to take possession of the life cycle. Rich observes how man has traditionally used female fertility to guarantee his own immortality. Through the birth of his children "he insures the disposition of his patrimony and the safe passage of his soul after death."[32]

Sedna attempts to galvanize Almira's power to create life free from patriarchal domination. "Almira the mystery of your womb makes you more powerful than that!" (86) But Almira rejects herself as a potential mother, claiming she is "too tired to have a baby."

Sedna envisions herself as the primeval link with the life process and describes the fertility of the lush sea landscape.

> When I was born, the sea held many marvellous creatures
> and nowhere was there a place more mysterious or a greater
> haven of life! And dotted throughout the seas were pools of
> shimmering sand, milky white crescents, where the creature
> came for rest, and to feed upon sweet dewy grasses, and
> mate; listening to the heavy grey roll of the sea. So many
> worlds there were! For three million years I have travelled
> and I have slept in a hundred islands. Islands appearing and
> disappearing...Now there is but one left. After that is gone
> there will be none.(86)

The disappearance of the landscape's magnificence parallels the evanescence of the matriarchal universe. Both appear barren and infertile. Almira still resists her obligation towards Sedna of accepting the fertility cycle. She begins to club Sedna, thinking she is a hallucination, and manages to pull off Sedna's headdress, discovering she is a woman inside. However, Almira hears George calling and decides to go to him, and, just as man turns his back on nature, Sedna is left abandoned on the beach. Sedna appeals to Almira's instinctive nature, "Life is precious to me…it once was to you." (87)

As symbolic of Almira's refusal to adopt Sedna's vision, she retreats to the cabin because it is "getting dark." (87) George intensifies this shrouded consciousness by declaring that soon she "won't be able to see." Sedna equates their blindness with the inability to reach enlightenment, and the closing of Almira's mind with the sun sinking into the darkness of night. "A darkness from which no light will be emitted ever!" (87) As Jones avows, through man's attempt to liberate himself from the natural forces which ultimately overpower him, he has diminished his own existence.

> As long as his defiance is radical, man shall remain an isolated voyager, a moving point on the map, surrounded by the threatening waves. Only when he is prepared to accept his final, if not immediate engulfment, shall he find comfort, love, communion.[33]

Sedna speaks out against the human corruption emanating from a cloistered vision. "You think you have power because you are human?" (88) Instead Sedna sees that man has only increased "the power of death!" Sedna appears on a rock, with her headpiece in one hand and an axe in the other, symbolic images of life and death. As she descends from the rock she dons the headpiece and asserts her belief in the life process. She rejects the distorted male stereotype of herself: "I am not a bare-breasted manifestation of a sex-starved fisherman. Mermaids indeed!" (88)

Almira finds Sedna's power disturbing, for Sedna is a frightening reminder of the deep truths she wishes to forget. Sedna provokes Almira's latency by scaring her with a raised axe, conveying the violence of mankind. "Here comes your darkness to cower and hide in. Run to George. Run from the sickness of men." (88) But Sedna, as a personification of nature's energy, innately trusts her omnipresence in the universe as being much superior to man's expression of power. "I know when they will live and when they will die!"

In Act II, Almira begins to awaken to the sublime genesis of nature. She feels her environment near the sea is suddenly "familiar," (89) and feels a deep connection, "as if I had lived here before." In contrast, George feels no such bond, unable to see any sign of life on the beach. "This place is empty!"..."Not even a clam to be found." (89) Almira herself describes the fertility of the sea and her incredible experience with Sedna. But George remains sceptical, representing man's inability to accept the magic of the natural world. George wants only to leave, threatened by the irrationality which opposes intellectual order. Entranced by Sedna's vision, Almira tells George she now has the power to carry on the campaign against the slaughter of the animal world built around the protection of the selkies. "By donating your time and money, we can ensure that selkies continue to live on this planet. No postage required for federal politicians." (91)

George, however, cannot accept Almira's vision of a mythical animal world. Now George has become disillusioned, claiming that the bureaucratic world will reject this mythical perception of animal life. "You're trying to save a hallucination." (90) George himself cannot accept this image of nature and perceives Almira's imaginative description as insanity. He is overcome with a sense of terror evoked by Almira's magical vision. "There is something out there! And it stinks. It's a putrid, rotting..." (91)

Sedna views George as a "poor pathetic creature." (92) He has become an image of the helpless figure of man, made more pitiful by his need to destroy and conquer nature in an attempt to alleviate his fear. Sedna appears to him as a rotting seal corpse, personifying his negative image of the natural world, one he must subdue. "I'll fix it Almira. There'll be no more seals." (92)

The portrayal of this double image of nature is a common theme in Canadian literature. The "two polarities of the state of mind"[34] in regard to nature is imbued by man's insignificance in the face of the life-affirming and destructive characteristics of nature, as Frye contends.

> At one pole of experience there is a fusion of human life and the life in nature; at the opposite pole is the identity of the sinister and terrible elements in nature with the death-wish in man.[35]

Sedna proclaims the absurdity of man's destructive impulse towards the natural domain, ironically calling him the "mighty protector of his family." (92) George kicks the corpse and Sedna cries out to him as her "Father." He is both the figure of her own father and the patriarchal God who transforms himself into her destroyer. Expressing a feminist awareness, Cowan relates this dichotomy to man's perception of woman. George massacres the corpse, merging the sensations of love and hate, illustrating man's ambivalent relationship with woman and nature. "Love you…(Silence.) Oh sweet mother of God…what have I done?" (93)

As part of the Woman-Nature metaphor, Sedna articulates the polarity of her double existence: "Half human, half seal. Each part of me hating the other." (93) On the one hand, Sedna experiences the victimization of the seal, and at the same time she is tormented by her human status which destroys animal life.

Sedna then appears to George as the old woman he met on the beach at the beginning of the play. She tells George he owes her a child for all the suffering man has caused. George, revealing his irresponsibility to nature, cries out in fear, "Nooooooo!!!"

In contrast, Sedna depicts the mystical and poetic inspiration of the natural world which inflames the imagination.

> The soul shall burst her fetters.
> At last and shall be free.
> As the sun, as the wind, as the night.
> As the stars, as the sea. (93)

Almira is transposed by this creative impression of nature. "Close your eyes. Open your ears. Listen. Just wave after wave, swelling, shattering, returning to the sea once again." (94) Engulfed by the sea, Almira unites with Sedna's vision. Sedna takes her to her home, a floating island in the sea and initiates Almira back into nature through ritual, placing a symbolic garland of seaflowers on her head. Together they dance, celebrating the unity of the human soul with the sensual world.

> The soul shall be crowned and calm
> Eyes fearless and she
> Shall be queen of the wind and the night
> Stars, sun, and sea. (95)

Sedna's vision evokes a female perception of nature, recalling the image of the Mother Goddess and an ancient fertility ritual. Feminist theologians like Daly, Christ and Ruether see Goddess worship as an important departure from patriarchal Judaic-Christian tradition, where female power is denied.

> The God/ess who is primal Matrix, the ground of being—
> new being, is neither stifling immanence nor rootless
> transcendence. Spirit and matter are not dichotomized but
> are inside and outside of the same thing.[36]

On an individual level, the symbol of the Goddess personifies the female "quest for authenticity and power."[37] The primeval union with "God/ess" inspires women's "authentic selves resurrected from under-neath the alienated self."[38] Through gazing in a mirror, Almira begins to recognize her own individuality and her female power of creation. However, she is afraid of self-knowledge as she must face the uncertainty of her existence. "I'm afraid of dreaming. I'm afraid of tomorrow and tomorrow. I'm losing my mind…I don't want to be alone." (95)

In contrast to the life-affirming ritual, Sedna recalls the destruction of the whales in the second world war, "their songs were mistaken for the sound of submarine sonar." (96) But the whales still sing, and like Sedna, they still have the instinct to create life. "New life is a wonder. And should be celebrated. A baby brings love into the world." Unlike the institution of motherhood described in *Ever Loving* and *Islands* where women's oppression is related to "the tyranny"[39] of human biology, Sedna's Divine Motherhood resonates Rich's rediscovery of motherhood "as experience," free from patriarchal control. Sedna interprets the fertility ritual of motherhood as a time of rejoicing, celebrating the wonder of female fertility: "For the great mystery that is ours." (98) About pre-patriarchal motherhood, the "Golden Age" Sedna mourns, Rich writes:

> Out of her body the woman created man, created woman, created continuing existence. Spiritualized into a divine being, she was the source of vegetation, fruition, fertility of every kind.[40]

Sedna makes a plea for the remembrance of the primeval "humble beginnings," (98) and offers Almira foods from the earth linked to female fertility, such as asparagus. This connection with the natural world through sensation reminds Almira of her erotic desires. She recalls George's smell, relating it to a "foreign market filled with unknown and forbidden scents."

Sedna reaffirms her belief in the life process, saying "the real pleasure in the world for men and women is still provided by children." (98) Almira points out, also, "the burden." Sedna calls for the transformation of patriarchal motherhood: "The work's in raising the husband not the children." (98)

Sedna unveils her relationship with her former husband to Almira. Prior to marriage she was an independent woman, "I refused every male that appeared at my doorstep." (99) However, she finally did succumb. "He told me he would cherish and honour me with a home and warmth and food. He also promised me a room of my own. So I married him." She reveals how her husband entrapped her, as the home turned out to be a domestic prison. In an attempt to liberate herself, she murdered her husband. Sedna's betrayal is portrayed in mythological terms as Sedna flees to her father's boat for protection, only to be sacrificed to the sea to pacify the anger of the gods. When she clings to the gunnels her father hacks off her fingers, which form into dolphins, seals, and the walrus. "Then from all around me, from my flesh and blood, were born the whales. They swam beneath my father's small dory till the sea boiled." (100)

By this reference to mythology, Sedna's resurrection into sea creatures signifies both her eternal connection with nature and her resistance of the patriarchal impulse to subjugate her.

> I rid myself of a husband who would have all my power drained in preparing his nest, his food, his clothes, and a father who bartered with my life. They prepared the scene for their own finish. (100)

The loss of Sedna's identity is symbolized by the extinction of the selkie species. Sedna does not feel Almira fully understands the sense of loss as Almira herself wishes her own species would disappear, one she calls "a deformed and demented race." (101) As she cannot comprehend the implications of this loss, Sedna transports her back to the beginning, before women's bond with nature was severed, when humanity and all living matter was integrated into "the Earth's Spirit."

Long ago,
The Earth's Spirit was everything.
That walked, swam, crawled
On her surface.
That bond is broken. (101)

Sedna re-enacts the broken bond between mankind and the animal world whereby Sedna becomes the seal and George personifies the hunter. George creeps around eyeing the seals, seeing them as objects to exploit. "Look at those mothers." (101) George ties Sedna with rope and calculates her value through her weight, becoming a savage and greedy hunter. "Throw the stone. Now. At the head. The head!" (102) George raises his axe to slay the seal. At this stage, Almira intervenes to prevent him, but Sedna wants Almira to see that her vision "is the nightmare you humans have spewed on this earth." (102)

A blackout occurs in the play and the sound of the sea is heard mingled with the protest cries of Almira, dissolving into the sound of soft waves lapping on the shore, followed by complete silence.

Sedna forces Almira to live through the nightmare in order to restore her sensitivity and willingness to fight the devastation of the animal kingdom. Almira is now conscious of the child growing inside her; the life force she embraces within. She asks Sedna for her guidance and wisdom in raising the child, and Sedna reassures her, "the sea will give you strength to bear the child." (105) Sedna wants the child to be raised as a selkie so that the "cycle would begin again!" (105) She becomes the child's Godmother, agreeing to share the child with Almira and George. Almira returns to the shack, and in the distance she hears the cry of the loons and ruminates about their deep loyalty, as loons bond forever. Sedna explains to Almira that their cries are so lonely because they recognize the bond that we have lost. "Union is a gift," (106) as most of life is spent divided from others. Sedna departs for the sea, leaving Almira with the reassurance that her vision will one day flame into being. "In waking and sleeping dreams, in joy, in love, a seed is planted. Dream us a new dream Almira." (107)

In the final scene of the play, George finds Almira still wearing the kimono Sedna gave her. In her disarray, she declares she almost stayed on the floating island with Sedna. George demonstrates his final acceptance of her vision by signing the letter for the protection of the selkies. "There are societies for the preservation of everything on this planet except for selkies and...ourselves." (108)

There is a sense of integration and enlightenment as Almira and George dance a waltz together. But again Almira smells the terrible odour. The rotting corpse, a symbol of man's exploitation of the animal world, will not let them forget. This image of destruction is juxtaposed with an image of rebirth and renewal. Almira feels the baby move inside her and imagines the power of the life force within her. "It's still there. The wind, and the waves, and the sounds of the sea." (110) Through this newly formed alliance with the natural world, Almira and George reinforce their own eternal bond, and like the loons, their expression of love merges with the sound of the waves.

Cindy Cowan gives new meaning to the Canadian literary search for a psychic rebirth in nature by correlating the female quest for identity with women's ancient power to create life. The Nova Scotia seashore, as the primeval lost Utopia, is ultimately regained through Almira's recognition of the omnipotent life process within her. As in *Islands* and *La Sagouine,* the protagonists pursue self-harmony in the healing powers of nature's eternal resources.

However, Cindy Cowan transposes the search for individual discovery into a new realm by envisioning nature as a metonym for the female biological process. Both *A Woman From the Sea* and *La Sagouine,* by depicting matriarchal power as the lost female identity, transport the female literary archetype into the medium of drama, transforming the myth of lost Paradise into a female dramatic mythology.

NOTES

1. Frye. p. 142.
2. Ibid. p. 245.
3. Ibid. p. 245.
4. Rich. p. 93.
5. Christ, Carol P. *Laughter of Aphrodite: Reflections on a Journey to the Goddess,* San Francisco: Harper and Row, 1987, p. 154.
6. Cowan, Cindy. "Introduction and Playwright's Notes," to *A Woman from the Sea,* in *Canadian Theatre Review* (Fall 1986) p. 63.
7. Ibid.
8. Ibid. p. 5.
9. Ibid. p. 63.
10. Ibid. p. 63.
11. Christ. p. 167.
12. Ibid. p. 166.
13. Frye. p. 242.
14. Ibid. p. 239.
15. Ibid. p. 240.
16. Atwood. *Survival,* p. 60.
17. Mitcham. p. 12.
18. Jones. p. 57.
19. Ibid.
20. Atwood. *Survival,* p. 79.
21. Ibid. p. 80.
22. Ruether. p. 83.
23. Ibid. p. 85.
24. Ibid. pp. 83-84.
25. Millett. p. 52.
26. Griffin, Susan. *Woman and Nature,* p. 168.
27. de Beauvoir. p. 162.
28. Jones. p. 51.
29. Ibid. p. 55.
30. Ibid. p. 58.
31. Ibid.
32. Rich. p. 64.
33. Jones. p. 127.
34. Kreisel. p. 256.
35. Frye. p. 246.
36. Ruether. p. 85.
37. Christ. p. 154.
38. Ruether. p. 71.
39. Firestone. p. 193.
40. Rich. p. 100.

Afterword

In their search for self-definition within the Canadian literary quest for identity, it has been shown that the five selected playwrights give a new dimension to Canadian theatre by interweaving the concepts of wilderness, immigration and imperialism into a dramatic female vision.

Wilderness, so dominant a myth in Canadian literature, acquires specific meaning to women, giving impetus to the imaginative interiorization of landscape as a metaphor for female consciousness, one which reflects both internal and external reality. The struggle for survival, the portrayal of woman as immigrant, and women's quest to survive alone in a male-defined environment, exemplifies women's marginality and search for social integration. Patriarchalism is interpreted in the plays as being consistent with imperial domination, through which women are excluded, and which leads to self-deprecating acceptance of masculine definitions against which women struggle for their individuality.

The playwrights in this study strive to enlarge female consciousness by voicing challenges to the conditions and traditions which have often alienated women from the mainstream of Canadian life. The uniqueness of their work springs from their faith in the value of women, and the conviction that they must question and clarify the assumptions about their position within the conventional frameworks of society.

Canadian women playwrights epitomize the female literary search for an "authentic language." The female struggle for self-definition is no more apparent than in the medium of drama, for, unlike the private world of fiction, drama, due to its public nature, has traditionally been a male domain. Taking their place in drama is a task that does not come without struggle. The socio-political repercussions have kept women silenced, carefully tucked away in a domestic cocoon. But more significant are the effects of this political silencing on the female psyche. In this state of inertia, the medium of drama was seen as too powerful, too spontaneous an expression for women who were conditioned to keep their feelings and ideas under control. For drama demands an intensity and honesty that has been denied women. Perhaps there was the fear that the masks would come off and women would reveal themselves, the way they really were, and all the centuries of contained emotions would come surging through. And women would remember their past connection with drama and ritual when their creative energy took center stage.

Gwen Pharis Ringwood writes how "fear of public condemnation"[1] kept women playwrights from writing about the complexities of female experience. She reveals how the political bias of patriarchy affected her own work.

> I know that I myself wrote plays for years withoutfully accepting the responsibilties I now feel must and should be accepted by a writer. I tried to write honestly but often chose material or forms that offered a self-protecting distancing. Often over the forty years I have wished for a pseudonym, guaranteeing anonymity so that my activities as writer could not impinge in any way on my family, my mother, my friends.[2]

Ringwood articulates the psychological confinement of women who try to express a dramatic vision in a patriarchal context. She sheds light on the

socio-political burdens which weighed heavily on the artistic consciousness of creative women throughout the ages and which, in Canada, stifled
the female imagination, leading to a lack of women playwrights. A report
by Rina Fraticelli shows that in 1981 only 10% of Canadian playwrights
were women. Fraticelli writes about the invalidation of the female
playwright's vision by mainstream society.

> In dismissing the substance of women's lives as insig-
> nificant, inappropriate, uninteresting and bland, the theory
> of gender discrimination finds its most efficient strategy.[3]

Margaret Hollingsworth also experienced the devaluing of female experience in her involovement in Canadian drama.

> The playwright is required to fight for her ideas and defend
> them in the forum of workshops, rehearsals, and, after the
> production, in the media. Her critics will be harsh, par-
> ticularly if she is a feminist playwright. [4]

Writing with a female language means that women will be challenging
the accepted, androcentric, vision of society. And the process of change, of
acknowledging an unfamiliar vision, is not always greeted favourably. The
period of transition is not without a struggle, for it requires a shift in
consciousness. It entails a re-evaluation of old forms and the transformation of accepted beliefs into new perceptions. But this metamorphosis will
lead to a more complete vision of human experience, one that accepts the
full range of women's aesthetic expression, a vision rooted in multi-levels
of being rather than the limitations of censorship and masculine bias.

Women playwrights, through the process of writing plays from a
female perspective, have begun the imaginative transformation that will
expand women's traditionally limited role in Canadian drama.

NOTES

1. Ringwood, Gwen Pharis. "Women and the Theatrical Tradition," *Atlantis,* (Fall 1978) p. 156.
2. Ibid. p. 156-7.
3. Fraticelli, Rina. "The Invisibility Factor—Status of Women in Canadian Theatre," *Fuse,* 6, no. 3 (September 1982) p. 13.
4. Hollingsworth, Margaret. "Why We Don't Write," *Canadian Theatre Review,*" 43 (Summer 1985) p. 22.

Bibliography

Primary Sources

Plays

Cowan, Cindy. *A Woman From the Sea,* in *Canadian Theatre Review,* (Fall 1986).

Hollingsworth, Margaret. *Ever Loving,* in *Willful Acts: Five Plays.* Toronto: The Coach House Press, 1985.

———. *Islands,* in *Willful Acts.*

Maillet, Antonine. *La Sagouine,* Toronto: Simon & Pierre, 1985.

Ravel, Aviva. *The Twisted Loaf,* Toronto: Playwrights Co-op, 1970.

Wylie, Betty Jane. *A Place on Earth,* Toronto: Playwrights Canada, 1982.

Secondary Sources

Anthony, Geraldine. *Stage Voices,* Toronto: Doubleday Canada Ltd. 1978.

Atwood, Margaret. "Afterword," *The Journals of Susanna Moodie,* Toronto: Oxford University Press, 1970, pp. 62-64.

Atwood, Margaret. *Survival,* Toronto: Anansi Press, 1972.

Beauvoir, Simone de. *The Second Sex,* New York: A.A. Knopf Inc. 1953, Vintage Books Edition, 1974.

Bessai, Diane. "Women, Feminism and Prairie Theatre," *Canadian Theatre Review,* 43 (Summer 1985) pp. 28-43.

———. "The Regionalism of Canadian Drama," *Canadian Literature,* 85 (Summer 1980) pp. 7-20.

Boag, Veronica Strong and Anita Clair Fellman. Eds. *Rethinking Canada: The Promise of Women's History,* Toronto: Copp Clark Pitman, 1986.

Bolt, Carol. "Female Leads: Search for Feminism in the Theatre,"*Canadian Forum,* (June/July 1987) pp. 37-40.

Brown, Cheryl L. and Karen Olsen. Eds. *Feminist Criticism: Essays on Theory, Poetry, and Prose,* Metuchen, N.J. and London: Scarecrow Press, Inc. 1978.

Chinoy, Helene Krich and Linda Walsh Jenkins. Eds. *Women in American Theatre,* New York: Crown Publishers, 1981.

Chopp, Rebecca S. *The Power to Speak: Feminism, Language, God,* New York: Cross Road Publishing, 1989.

Christ, Carol P. *Laughter of Aphrodite: Reflections on a Journey to the Goddess,* San Fransisco: Harper and Row, 1987.

Conolly, L.W. Ed. *Canadian Drama and the Critics,* Vancouver: Talonbooks, 1987.

Cook, Ramsay and Wendy Mitchison. Eds. *The Proper Sphere: Woman's Place in Canadian Society,* Toronto: Oxford University Press, 1976.

Firestone, Shulamith. *The Dialectic of Sex: The Case for Feminist Revolution,* New York: Morrow, 1970.

Fraticelli, Rina. "The Invisibility Factor—Status of Women in Canadian Theatre," *Fuse,* 6, no. 3 (September 1982) pp. 112-124.

Frye, Northrop. *The Bush Garden: Essays on the Canadian Imagination,* Toronto: Anansi Press, 1971.

Griffin, Susan. *Rape: Woman and Nature,* New York: Harper and Row, 1978.

———. *The Power of Consciousness,* New York: Harper and Row, 1979.

Hallen, Patsy. "Making Peace with the Environment: Why Ecology Needs Feminism," *Canadian Woman Studies,* 9, no. 1 (Spring 1988) pp. 9-18.

Holden, John. "Please, More Comedies," *Curtain Call,* 9, on. 1, (October 1937) p. 4.

Hollingsworth, Margaret. "Why We Don't Write," *Canadian Theatre* Review, 43 (Summer 1985) pp. 21-27.

Howells, Coral Ann. *Private and Fictional Words: Canadian Women Novelists of the 1970s and 1980s,* London and New York: Methuen, 1987.

Janeway, Elizabeth. *Man's World Woman's Place: A Study in Social Mythology,* New York: Morrow, 1971.

Jones, Douglas G. *Butterfly on Rock: A Study of Themes and Images in Canadian Literature,* Toronto: University of Toronto Press, 1970.

Keyssar, Helene. *Feminist Theatre: An Introduction to Plays of Contemporary British and American Women,* London: MacMillan Publishers Ltd. 1984.

Kreisel, Henry. "The Prairie: A State of Mind," *Contexts of Canadian Criticism*, ed. Eli
    Mandel, Chicago: University of Chicago Press, 1971, pp. 254-266.

Lerner, Gerda. *The Female Experience*, Indianapolis: Bobbs-Merrill Co. Inc. 1977.

Lips, Hilary M. "Women and Power: Psychology's Search for New Directions," *Atlantis*,
    5, no. 1 (Fall 1979) pp. 1-13.

Lushington, Kate. "Fear of Feminism," *Canadian Theatre Review*, 43 (Summer 1985)
    pp. 5-11.

Malpede, Karen. Ed. *Women in Theatre: Compassion and Hope*, New York: Drama Books
    Publishers, 1983.

Marks, Elaine and Isabelle de Coutivron. Eds. *New French Feminisms: An Anthology*,
    Amherst: University of Massachusetts Press, 1980.

McClung, Nellie. *The Stream Runs Fast*, 1945. Reissued by Thomas Allen Ltd. 1965.

Miles, Angela R. and Geraldine Finn. Eds. *Feminism in Canada*, Montreal: Black Rose
    Books, 1982.

Miller, Jean Baker. *Toward a New Psycholgy of Women*, Boston: Beacon Press, 1976.

Millett, Kate. *Sexual Politics*, Garden City, N.J: Doubleday, 1970.

Mitcham, Allison. *The Northern Imagination: A Study of Northern Canadian Literature*,
    Moonbeam, Ontario: Penumbra Press, 1983.

Moi, Toril. *Sexual/Textual Politics*, London: Methuen, 1985.

Moore, Mavor. "Cultural Myths and Realities," *Canadian Theatre Review*, 34 (Spring 1982)
    pp. 23-27.

Morley, Patricia. "Talking with Aviva Ravel, on Priorities, Fairness, and Being Human,"
    Canadian Drama, (Fall 1979) pp. 179-188.

Moss, John George. *Patterns of Isolation in English Canadian Fiction*, Toronto: McClelland
    and Stewart, 1974.

New, William H. *Dramatists in Canada*, Vancouver: University of British Columbia Press,
    1985.

Newton, Judith and Deborah Rosenfelt. Eds. *Feminist Criticism and Social Change: Sex,
    Class, and Race in Literature and Culture*, New York and London: Methuen, 1985.

Oberman, Sheldon and Elaine Newton. *Mirror of a People: Canadian Jewish Experience in
    Poetry and Prose*, Winnipeg: Jewish Educational Publishers of Canada Inc. 1985.

Perkyns, Richard. Ed. *Major Plays of the Canadian Theatre 1934-1984*, Toronto: Irwin
    Publishing, 1984.

Plant, Richard. Ed. *Modern Canadian Drama*, Markham, Ontario: Penguin Books Canada,
    1984.

Pollock, Sharon. "Canada's Playwrights: Finding their Place," *Canadian Theatre Review*,
    34 (Spring 1982) pp. 34-38.

Rabine, Leslie Wahl. "A Feminist Politics of Non-Identity," *Feminist Studies*, 14, no. 1 (Spring 1988) pp. 11-31.

Radicalesbians. "The Woman-Identified Woman," *Radical Feminism*, ed. Anne Koedt, New York: Quadrangle Books, 1973, pp. 240-245.

Rich, Adrienne. *Of Woman Born: Motherhood as Experience and Institution*, New York: W.W. Norton and Co. Inc. 1976.

Ringwood, Gwen Pharis. "Women and the Theatrical Tradition," *Atlantis*, 4, no. 1 (Fall 1978) pp. 154-158.

Rossiter, Amy. *From Private to Public: A Feminist Exploration of Early Mothering*, Toronto: Women's Press.

Rubin, Don. "Celebrating the Nation: History and the Canadian Theatre," *Canadian Theatre Review*, 34 (Spring 1982) pp. 12-22.

Ruether, Rosemary Radford. *Sexism and God-Talk: Toward a Feminist Theology*, Boston: Beacon Press, 1983.

Russell, Diana E.H. "The Nuclear Mentality: An Outgrowth of the Masculine Mentality," *Atlantis*, 12, no. 2 (Spring 1987) pp. 10-16.

Ryga, George. "Contemporary Theatre and its Language," *Canadian Theatre Review*, 14 (Spring 1977) pp. 4-9.

————. "The Need for a Mythology," *Canadian Theatre Review*, 16 (Fall 1977) pp. 4-6.

Sedgwick, Eve Kosofsky. *Between Men: English Literature and Male Homosocial Desire*, New York: Columbia University Press, 1985.

Shteir, Ann B. Ed. *Women on Women*, Toronto: Gerstein Lecture Series, York University, 1976.

Singer, June. *Androgyny: Toward a New Theory of Sexuality*, Garden City, N.J: Anchor Press, 1976.

Spacks, Patricia Meyer. *The Female Imagination*, New York: Avon Books, 1975.

Stacey, Margaret and Marion Price. *Women, Power, and Politics*, London: Tavistock Publications, 1981.

Stephenson, Marylee. Ed. *Women in Canada*, Don Mills, Ontario: General Publishing Co. Ltd. 1977.

Storrie, Kathleen. Ed. *Women: Isolation and Bonding*, Toronto: Methuen, 1987.

Sullivan, Rosemary. "Beyond Survival," *Canadian Forum*, (March 1978) pp. 6-7.

Trofimenkoff, Susan Mann. "Nationalism, Feminism and Canadian Intellectual History," *Canadian Literature*, 83 (Winter 1979) pp. 7-20.

Usmiani, Renate. *Second Stage: The Alternative Theatre Movement in Canada*, Vancouver: University of British Columbia Press, 1983.

Wagner, Anton. Ed. *Canada's Lost Plays: Women Pioneers,* vol. 2, Toronto: Canadian Theatre Review Publications, 1979.

Wagner, Anton. "From Art to Theory: Canada's Critical Tools," *Canadian Theatre Review,* 34 (Spring 1982) pp. 59-83.

———. Ed. *Contemporary Canadian Theatre: New World Visions,* Toronto: Simon and Pierre, 1985.

Wallace, Robert and Cynthia Zimmerman. Eds. *The Work: Conversations with English-Canadian Playwrights,* Toronto: The Coach House Press, 1982.

Wandor, Michelene. *Carry on, Understudies: Theatre and Sexual Politics,* London and New York: Routledge and Kegan Paul, 1986.

Watchel, Eleanor, "British Columbia: Two Steps Backward from the One Step Forward," *Canadian Theatre Review,* 43 (Summer 1985) pp. 12-20.

APHRA BEHN
The English Sappho
by George Woodcock

All women together ought to let flowers fall on the tomb of Aphra Behn, for it was she who earned them the right to speak their minds.
Virginia Woolf

...a valuable introduction to this remarkable woman who was a pioneer feminist, free spirit, liberated woman and professional writer during the Restoration.
Ottawa Citizen

Aphra Behn holds a unique place in history. Pioneer of women's emancipation, anticipator of abolitionism, advocate of free marriage, precursor of Rousseau, and inventor of much that has become permanent in the English novel as it has developed since her time, as well as author of some of the best songs and plays in English, she holds a place second to none of her contemporaries in history.

George Woodcock analyzes each of Behn's plays and novels. He also deals with the politics of the English Restoration: the break with Puritanism and Cromwell; the revival of the House of Stuart; the triumph of parliament in the so-called "Great Revolution" and the resulting verbal battles between Whigs and Tories.

George Woodcock has been variously described as "quite possibly the most civilized man in Canada," "a great human being," and "a kind of John Stuart Mill of dedication to intellectual excellence and the cause of human liberty."
Toronto Star

248 pages
Paperback ISBN: 0-921689-40-3 $16.95
Hardcover ISBN: 0-921689-41-1 $36.95

FINDING OUR WAY
Rethinking Eco-Feminist Politics
by Janet Biehl

Inundated by advocates of "cultural feminism,"Goddess worship, deep ecology, and post-modernism, today's eco-feminist movement has lost much of its critical and constructive voice. In *Finding Our Way*, feminist theorist Janet Biehl lays the groundwork for a new left eco-feminist politics.

In four essays, Biehl explores eco-feminism's intellectual affinities with social ecology and other schools of thought; critiques the increasing role of Goddess mythology within today's movement; defends reason and naturalism against what she sees as a "counter-Enlightenment" mentality within feminist and academic circles; and mines the Western democratic tradition for its relevant political insights for feminists today.

Finding Our Way is must reading for anyone wishing to explore the philosophical connections between feminism, ecology, and the left.

210 pages
Paperback ISBN: 0-921689-78-0 $13.95
Hardcover ISBN: 0-921689-79-9 $32.95

FEMINISM

edited by
Angela Miles and Geraldine Finn

2nd edition

...a very satisfying book...the articles are highly readable, well argued, stimulating, and provocative...the volume as a whole is remarkable for its thematic coherence...What is striking about this book is that the authors...embark upon a stimulating and insightful, though hazardous, task of providing an alternative feminist framework to guide how scholarship and politics should be carried out...deserves to be read widely.
Canadian Journal of Political Science

Provides a wide range of readings...[F]eminist theories which threaten a reversion of the status quo, such as the one espoused here, sharpen our perspective on other analyses. Many articles concerning research point to the ways this might be accomplished.
Canadian Review of Sociology

An anthology of signal essays by leading feminist scholars. The articles in this collection deal with fundamental questions of theory and practice, the relation between the world of academia and the world of activism, and the development of feminist theory. This new edition includes several exciting new articles, including contributions from Nicole Brossard, Anne Cameron, Linda Christiansen-Ruffman, Kathleen A. Lahey, and the singing group Four the Moment.

400 pages
Paperback ISBN: 0-921689-22-5 $19.95
Hardcover ISBN: 0-921689-23-3 $39.95

WOMEN AND COUNTER-POWER

edited by Yolande Cohen

...these scholarly essays document women's political activity in antiestablishment movements, both historical and recent, in some of the nations peripheral to the powerful Western democracies and the USSR; Spain, Italy, Canada, Argentina, Algeria, Portugal, and Poland...The Authors' ...material provides information, as well as insights, not readily available elsewhere.
Small Press

This book contributes to the debate on the many aspects of women's participation.
Le Devoir

Each author presents not only the historical importance of the women's struggle, but also its contradictions and ambivalence.
Espace, Population et Société

Essays by scholars and activists compare the experiences of women in various countries: the significance of women's work in voluntary associations (Italy and Canada), in writing (France), under military dictatorship (Argentina), and during a war of national liberation (Algeria), in Solidarnösc (Poland). This is a fresh vision of the emancipation of women in sweeping international scope.

244 pages
Paperback ISBN: 0-921689-10-1   **$19.95**
Hardcover ISBN: 0-921689-11-X   **$39.95**

BLACK ROSE BOOKS

has also published the following related titles:

FEMINISM, *edited by Angela Miles and Geraldine Finn*

MOTHER WAS NOT A PERSON, *edited by Margaret Andersen*

THINGS WHICH ARE DONE IN SECRET, *by Marlene Dixon*

WOMEN AND COUNTER-POWER, *edited by Yolande Cohen*

WOMEN AND REVOLUTION, *edited by Lydia Sargent*

LOUISE MICHEL, *by Edith Thomas*

BATTERED WOMEN, *by Micheline Beaudry*

THE REGULATION OF DESIRE: Sexuality in Canada, *by Gary Kinsman*

SEX AND GERMS: The Politics of AIDS, *by Cindy Patton*

OSCAR WILDE: The Double Image, *by George Woodcock*

THE WRITER AND POLITICS, *by George Woodcock*

RUSSIAN LITERATURE: Ideals and Realities, *by Peter Kropotkin, Introduction by George Woodcock*

WILLIAM GODWIN: A Biographical Study, *by George Woodcock*

THE ANARCHIST PAPERS 1, *edited by Dimitrios Roussopoulos*

THE ANARCHIST PAPERS 2, *edited by Dimitrios Roussopoulos*

THE ANARCHIST PAPERS 3, *edited by Dimitrios Roussopoulos*

send for a free catalogue of all our titles

BLACK ROSE BOOKS

P.O. Box 1258

Succ. Place du Parc

Montréal, Québec

H3W 2R3 Canada

Printed by
the workers of
Editions Marquis, Montmagny, Que.
for
Black Rose Books Ltd.

2352